HISTORIC
COLUMBUS
TAVERNS

HISTORIC
COLUMBUS
TAVERNS

The Capital City's Most Storied Saloons

Tom Betti & Doreen Uhas Sauer
for Columbus Landmarks Foundation

Charleston — London

THE
History
PRESS

Published by The History Press
Charleston, SC 29403
www.historypress.net

Cover images courtesy of Columbus Metropolitan Library Image Collections, Columbus Jewish Historical Society, Ohio State Journal, Sam Betti and Tom Betti.

First published 2012

Manufactured in the United States

ISBN 978.1.60949.670.8

Library of Congress CIP data applied for.

Dedicated to the volunteers of the Columbus Landmarks Foundation.
Without you, nothing would be easy.

Contents

Acknowledgements

Columbus, Ohio, is home to one of the best library systems in the United States, the Columbus Metropolitan Library, as evidenced by its many national awards. Historic research would not be possible without the extensive collections and the exemplary staff. Special thanks to Nick Taggert and Julie Callahan for never saying no and for always helping to play detectives and research wranglers.

Thank you to Teresa Carsten (Nellie Kampmann), Sandy Lehman, Terry Sherburn, Ed Lentz, and Conrade Hindes for their scholarly research and generous sharing. Special note to all of the Columbus Landmarks Foundation's Education Committee for their volunteer time, good ideas and diligence: Anne Seren, Barb Hackman, David Binkovitz, Terry Sherburn, Sandy Lehman, Conrade Hindes, Teresa Carsten (Nellie Kampmann), Becky Ellis, Cathy Appel, Sherry Walls, Stu Koblentz, John Seren, Cathy Nelson, Erin Reynolds and Amanda Nelson. Thank you to Kathy Mast Kane and Becky West for encouragement.

And our continued thanks to the owners, bartenders, waitstaff and managers who support Columbus Landmarks Foundation's programming in many ways: Liz Lessner, the Jury Room; Marte Dobosh, Paul Kroll and Paul Marazzo, the Athletic Club of Columbus; Michael Berton, Westin Great Southern Hotel; Roger McLane, the Flat Iron; Lenny Kolada and Michael, Char-Bar; Davino Natinsky and Rick, Club Diversity; Jim Talbot and family, Main Bar; Richard Stopper, Level; Sue and Tim Gall, Maennerchor and Hey-Hey; Adrian Rosu, Ringside; Richard Stevens, Elevator; Lenny Kolada, Barley's; Patrick Melick, Mac's Café; Randy Corbin, Little Palace; and the management team of Club 185.

In addition, thank you, Joe Gartrell of The History Press. Cheers to you!

Special thanks to Tom's parents, Sam and Lena Betti, and sister, Gina, for their support, and a warm acknowledgement to Kelan and Amanda Craig, Skylar Branstool, Theresa Larson, Francine Smith, Anne Saunier and Judge George C. Smith. Special acknowledgement to Dave Pagnard and Randy Cole for encouragement, Neal Larrimer for contributions, John Sauer for editing and the Board of Columbus Landmarks Foundation for support. Thank you to the Sauers and the Quickerts for the best stories, generously shared and always quotable.

Photo credits: Columbus Metropolitan Library Image Collections (CML), Billy Ireland Collection at The Ohio State University, Billy Ireland Cartoon Library & Museum (OSUCL), Columbus Jewish Historical Society (CJHL), the *Columbus Dispatch* (*CD*), *Columbus Citizen Journal* (*CCJ*), *Ohio State Journal* (*OSJ*), Sam Betti (SB), Tom Betti (TB), Private Collection (PC) and Ohio Environmental Protection Agency (EPA).

Introduction

Take This, Elise!

From the beginning, there was always a gimmick.
—*John Mariani,* America Eats Out, *1991*

Inns, taverns and saloons often played a prominent role in the history and affairs of the United States. They were backdrops to the political, social and economic events of their day—no doubt, a legacy of the English fondness for grog and talk, beer and informed (or low informed) argument. And since the sports bar had not been invented yet, politics was both the participatory and spectator sport of the day.

Thomas Jefferson worked on the Declaration of Independence in the Indian Queen Tavern in Philadelphia. Many patriotic revolutionary plans were plotted in Massachusetts taverns owned by not-so-loyal-to-the-King tavern keepers. The Whig Party's headquarters were in a Boston tavern, and the Ohio Land Company, which helped to open Ohio to development, started in another Boston tavern, the Bunch of Grapes. Even today, some young scholars of American history are astonished to that learn Samuel Adams is not just a beer, but also a real man and a Patriot.

Columbus's early historic taverns and saloons—inns, hotels, dives and assorted watering holes—are not part of the revered traditions of colonial inns. As establishments on the westernmost edge of settlement and into the late nineteenth century, Columbus's taverns and inns, however, did enjoy some of the novelties of eating out and the foodie trends of their day—for instance, the emergence of the coffeehouse (which did not just sell coffee); the novel use of napkins (rare in America before 1850); displays of gimmicks or come-ons (a bear?); and the emergence of the oyster house (ask yourself: Would you eat an oyster in nineteenth-century Columbus?)

The food in early Columbus taverns, hotels and coffeehouses was basic frontier fare, and it probably did not compare to the piles of turkey, sweet potatoes, puddings and New England regional dishes of the eastern seaboard. But the drinks might have been comparable—rum, brandy, hard cider, whiskey, beer and something that is described as "resembling gin."

Columbus had retail distilleries (and probably many homemade versions) in nearby Clinton and Mifflin Townships within the first few years of its establishment. Distilleries were a handicraft industry, and the making of alcoholic beverages would not be considered an industry until the emergence of the German breweries after the Civil War. Distilleries were important because they were a way to keep grain crops from rotting.

Columbus taverns and inns were places for men to gather to drink, often heavily. Wives, widows and children often worked in taverns. While not exclusive to men, taverns and saloons, by the end of the nineteenth century, were gentlemen's clubs because the Victorian era dictated a more pronounced separation between men's and women's activities.

Early taverns were places vital to the civic life of a young community—gathering spots, rallying points, reading rooms, de facto news offices and common rooms with heat in the winter and flies in the summer. The term "tavern" was not well defined. Anyone who opened a door or provided a meal and drink was operating a tavern. If he or she added a place to sleep, it was an inn.

So integral was the tavern or inn (and here should be added "saloon") to the life of the community that it was not incidental or accidental that many village would-be politicians or their family members were often the operators of the establishments. What better place to hear the news of the day? Become part of early city planning? Understand where the money and taxes were coming from and going to? Learn which way the winds of business, agriculture and politics were blowing?

An early Wisconsin pioneer commented in a letter back home that the way to make a village was to have two or three dozen people agree to put up houses and, if possible, a store or a post office—and there must be a tavern. For Columbus, founded to be a state capital, the close association of taverns and courts underscored the necessity of having a place to provide housing for lawyers, judges or litigants and also the need to make a tavern into a courtroom. In the early days of Columbus, the tavern was even where Mass was served for the Catholic community.

Artist drawing of High Street in 1846. Pictured on the right is the first Neil House and American House Hotel. The first statehouse is on the left. *CML.*

And since Columbus's location in the center of the state was so dependent on good roads and reliable conveyances, the decision makers who used the tavern as a civic center provided lubrication as useful as the grease on the wheels of a buckboard.

The decision to improve the Granville Road (the Dublin Granville Road, today's Route 161), the most direct eastern road into Columbus and one continuous mudhole, was decided in a tavern. Some of the most important citizens of Franklin County—William Neil, John Kerr and Samuel Flenniken—met with citizens of Licking County on April 11, 1823, at the tavern of Robert Russell, between Columbus and Granville, to plan for their May workdays on the road.

Likewise, the political stars of their day held court at Columbus's Golden Bell tavern across from the first Statehouse two years later in 1825. The famous governor of New York, Dewitt Clinton, escorted by a squadron of cavalry, light artillery, a rifle corps, the governor of Ohio and many of the governor's closest friends, officially celebrated the opening of the canal into Columbus (near the present site of Waterford Tower). Clinton, the promoter of New York's canals, most notably the Erie Canal, congratulated Ohio on its fertility (its land, not citizens), predicted the canal's revenue would yield at least a million dollars in ten years and participated in a grand dinner with many toasts (alcohol, not bread).

However, within ten years, Columbus did not reap a million in income—it reaped cholera, with about two hundred deaths in a city of three thousand, and many residents fled to Mount Vernon and Chillicothe. What came after that? Certainly not a rush to the river to toast. More taverns.

And yes, it is said that the final decision of where to locate Ohio's capital—Chillicothe, Delaware, Worthington, Zanesville or Columbus—was debated and decided in a tavern. Alcohol and offers of money and land to build a state capital and a penitentiary by Franklinton founder Lucas Sullivant and others cinched the deal.

Reportedly, Columbus was born in a tavern—the city, not the explorer.

So, where are the historic taverns and colorful saloons of old Columbus?

In 1926, Elise Lathrope, wrote *Early American Inns and Taverns*, an old standard on the history of such establishments. The promotion for the book reported it to be very complete:

> *From the Atlantic to the Pacific, from Mexico to Canada, in fact from every state of the Union, the author has gathered the romance and historic story of more than thirteen hundred early American Inns and Taverns—a narrative unique in the literature of early American days. The book will be found inclusive, authoritative, and definitive…the author has realized to the full the picturesque drama of old posting days, and has recreated this romantic and colorful past.*

And Elise does deliver—history, hauntings, murder, elopement, secret meetings and plots abound. Charles Dickens, nineteenth-century English novelist on his tour of America, seems to have visited more taverns in her book than the never-ending journey-taker Henry Clay, the Kentucky statesman, who visited home in Ashland, Kentucky, only long enough to sire more children.

Her chapter on Ohio includes ninety-five taverns that were seventy-five years or older in 1926, including those in well-known communities already established by the mid-nineteenth century—Cleveland, Painesville, Zanesville, Cambridge and Washington—and along lesser-known stops, like Elizabethtown, Hendrysburg and Fultonham. There are twenty-two taverns in or near Cambridge, Ohio. Her lists include picturesque-sounding tavern names like the Blue Lion and the Sign of the Orange Tree (Zanesville) and O.K. House (Champaign County).

However, maybe she felt Columbus did not have the romance and colorful past of say, Xenia's Log Tavern (ok, no evocative name here), which she writes about—but Elise just does not deliver in the capital city.

Out of 1,300 listings, Elise Lathrop lists only one tavern in Columbus—the "Neal House." Oh, the horror—one tavern—and it is spelled wrong.

Despite the fact that Columbus's growth and economic stability—and indeed its tavern and inn trades—were based on its location as a crossroads,

Right: William Neil started Columbus to Chillicothe mail delivery in 1822, co-founded the Neil Moore stagecoach line and was later associated with railroads. Perhaps his most famous business was the Neil House Hotel, a Columbus tradition from 1840 to 1980. *CML.*

Below: Bott Brothers was a lavish men's saloon that offered billiards and a cigar and candy shop, as well as alcohol and food. It still exists today at 161 North High Street as the Elevator Brewery and Draught Haus. *CML.*

Elise seems to have missed the (canal) boat. Metaphorically, she also missed the stagecoach that made a fortune for William Neil (not Neal), the first trains out of Xenia, the National Road that spurred the growth of more taverns and all of the more than 120 daily railroad departures and arrivals of the early twentieth century. To torture the metaphor a little more, in her own time, she even missed the Columbus transportation link to the first land-air cross transcontinental system that created Port Columbus in the 1920s. Surely, she could have enjoyed a Harvey Wallbanger somewhere near the terminal.

Elise, this book is for you because you clearly missed a good time in not visiting Columbus's historic taverns. Writing in 1926, Elise, you should have stayed to enjoy the roadhouses, private clubs, dives, neighborhood bars, the speakeasies and the return of the breweries after Prohibition.

And this modest history of Columbus is for all the tour-takers and would-be tour-takers on Columbus Landmarks Foundation's Historic Tavern Tours and Historic Haunted Tavern Tours who wanted more stories, more background on the remnants of architecture and artifacts, more sense of place, more understanding of a city celebrating its 200th birthday and more connections to Columbus's "liquid assets."

Chapter 1
Taverns of the "Infant City"

Beer, Barristers, Baths and a Bear

Now let them drink till they nod and wink
Even as good fellows should do;
They shall not miss to have the bliss
Good ale doth bring men to.
—Seventeenth-century English toast, attributed to John Still

Ordered that a license be granted William Domigan Sr. to keep tavern in
his own house in Franklinton until the next Court of Common Pleas for
Franklin County, and afterward he can renew his license…Ordered that
license be granted Joseph Foos to keep a tavern at the house occupied by him
in Franklinton for the accommodation of travelers until the next Court of
Common Pleas for Franklin County, and afterward until the license can be
renewed.
—Lucas Sullivant, Franklin County court record, 1803

Tavern and inn were synonymous in eighteenth-century America—a must for the traveler, but also a place for community gathering. A tavern in Franklinton and early Columbus—and the drink it dispensed—was social event, hostel and refuge, city government, public amenity and health food store, as beer and spirits were more reliable and healthful to drink than the water.

Tavern keeping was a potentially lucrative business with little investment of overhead required. Contrary to European inn keeping customs, the American tavern or inn generally kept the latchstring out because

Americans had less regard for privacy on the frontier—and less room to provide privacy. Eating, sleeping, drinking and entertainment all happened in one or two rooms—so did smoke inhalation, lack of temperature control and sometimes chaotic socializing among traders, newlyweds, drovers, foreigners, dogs, land speculators, young children, pregnant women, surveyors, servants and itinerant preachers.

Because the settlement of Franklinton, established in 1797 on the west side of the Scioto River, predated the founding of Columbus, Franklinton deserves the honor of having the first local tavern—and since Franklinton has been a neighborhood in Columbus since the 1870s, it should also be able to claim the first neighborhood bar.

However, whose tavern was the first is a question open to debate. Historians differ, and many families' log dwellings became de facto early taverns, altered to handle overnight guests or to provide food and drink.

Taverns depended on customers, and situated on the edge of what was considered the frontier, Franklinton was already on established crossroads used by Native Americans. Running north and south through the Scioto River valley was the well-known Scioto Trail, or Warrior's Trail, connecting the Ohio River and the portage of the Sandusky River to northern Ohio. Linking Franklinton from the east were the Moravian Trail (from the area above Zoar), the Mongahela Trail (from the Ohio River near Pittsburgh) and the Mingo Trail (which followed the Muskingham River). The Miami Trail originated in northwestern Ohio and connected Franklinton to the western lands of the Maumee River and the Black Swamp.

However, the crossroads leading into Franklinton were almost impassable. They were paths wide enough for only horses or mules. There were no pleasure carriages within a hundred miles of Columbus and no bridges. The Ohio legislature gave a carrier three days to carry election materials from Columbus to Chillicothe. Most people arrived by canoe, and the river was declared navigable by the legislature in 1808. In 1810, the first barges were loaded with goods to sell in New Orleans markets. This was the primary route used by travelers looking to settle in Central Ohio or move even further west.

The conditions of early roads were enough to make a man or mule want to drink. Columbus was truly a frontier.

The Scott Tavern was described as a "place of public entertainment." Built by James Scott in 1802, one year before Ohio became a state, "house of entertainment" meant that it welcomed both travelers and residents, and though there might be occasional music or gaming, drinkers were more apt to entertain themselves.

The Capital City's Most Storied Saloons

Four Mile House Inn and Tavern at 2904 West Broad Street was a stop for wagon travelers. The size and scale of the tavern was consistent with other early taverns at this time. *CML.*

Was his tavern the first? Scott is credited with the first "grocery" store, and his tavern and grocery were, most likely, one and the same. Presumably, it was along present-day West Broad Street and possibly close to the center of the town's activity but pulled back from the periodic flooding of the river, somewhere between Mill and Washington Streets (now the Sandusky interchange).

James Scott, like Franklinton's founder, Lucas Sullivant, was a surveyor and had charge of surveying the John Dunlap tract of four thousand acres up the Whetstone River (now Olentangy River). The tract had been sold to Jonathan Dayton and Jonas Stanbury in 1802 and was part of a tract purchased by James Kilbourne and others for the settlement of Worthington.

Colonel Kilbourne commented on the importance of Scott's tavern:

> *On Friday, May 6 (1803) at evening arrived at Franklinton very wet, cold, and much fatigued. Put up at James Scott's Esq, the man who had the care of survey for the Dunlap section. Sat. May 7th. Left Franklinton, went up Whetstone, and spent this and the two following days in the woods viewing our lands, and choosing out a place most favorable for our first improvement. Returned to Franklinton Monday evening the 9th and found there the Wm Morrisons, who had arrived there the evening before…and put up with him at Scotts.*

John Kerr's Land Office, as seen in 1892, in Franklinton. Both Kerr and Sullivant helped to settle Franklinton with lots. *CML.*

Surveying four thousand acres presumably meant putting down one's roots because Scott's tavern lasted for some time. Surveying was physically hard work and subject to the deprivations of continuous camping and pay of less than a dollar a day. And there was always a sense of fearful anticipation of when the other shoe (or, in this case, the other moccasin) would drop. Native Americans and early settlers, who had been wary of each other since the defeat of the tribes in 1794 at the Battle of Fallen Timbers, would remain so for the next twenty years through the War of 1812.

The Scott tavern appears to be well known but was not the only tavern in the area. Franklinton, settled by Virginians and Kentuckians whose native states had been famous for distilleries and bourbons, was no dry town. While some early settlers who had been part of the original Lucas Sullivant surveying party of the 1790s came as farmers, carpenters and blacksmiths, other Franklinton settlers arrived with the tavern business already in their blood—like William Domigan, from Maryland, and David Broderick.

Joseph Foos and wife, Lydia Nelson Foos, who came from Kentucky in 1798, are also credited with being the first tavern keepers in Franklinton— perhaps because they had a real license to operate and four dollars to pay the fee. Taverns were granted licenses by a common pleas judge to sell alcoholic beverages and accommodate travelers. Foos would become one of the first of three such judges in Franklin County when Ohio became a state in 1803.

Foos had an unusual life. He had been lured to Ohio by Lucas Sullivant to become an early settler, but, at thirty years of age, Foos had almost no education. He turned his tavern into his private schoolhouse, striking a bargain with a penniless Irish former schoolmaster—room and board for tutoring. He was a good enough student to become a judge, and in 1808, he became a state senator where he served for almost twenty years. In the War of 1812, Foos became a volunteer and worked his way to brigadier general. Judge Foos also ran a ferry service on the Scioto from Franklinton to Columbus, and he is credited as being the one who gave the city of Columbus its name, in honor of another boatman, Christopher Columbus. Foos's life is a lesson in how tavern keeping was all about social networking and career advancement.

When Foos and William Domigan were granted licenses in 1803, the term used was "operating a tavern." In 1804, court records for both men show that the word "tavern" changed to "house of public entertainment."

In these same 1804 court records of Franklin County are other topics of legislation worth noting because they show the issues of the day and what the courts were thinking about—new taverns (now to be licensed by a governing body), regulation of transportation regarding the increased number of travelers on the roads (and the subsequent new revenue streams in tolls) and establishments that would give the appearance of community order and/or manage lawbreakers (errant travelers, drunks or drive-off toll evaders).

Licenses to keep taverns (or places of entertainment) were granted to Ezra Griswold of Worthington, whose Griswold Tavern lasted into the twentieth century; William Harper, of Harrison Township; Nathan Carpenter, of Liberty Township; and Mrs. Elizabeth Whitaker, who may have lived in Franklinton. Toll collectors or "viewers of roads" were appointed, and the building of a

Reverend James Hoge, a pillar of the Franklinton community who oversaw much of Franklinton and early Columbus, was reported to be Columbus's only non-tavern goer. *CML*.

jail was to be done "immediately" for the county. The jail was built of twelve-foot logs—exactly spelled out to thickness, placement and construction. It required strong shutters and windows with iron bars.

In 1812, when Columbus was established, commerce began to migrate from the west side of the river to the new borough on the east side. Columbus was little more than an intersection of paths, with only a few cleared plots near Broad and High and at Front Street. It must have been raw—promising but unimproved land. There was a small field and a cabin near the river where Rich Street would have terminated at the Scioto and a cabin and garden belonging to John Brickell, a former Indian captive, near where the Ohio Penitentiary stood (now North Bank Park). To the south was a field past an extraordinarily large Indian mound (thus giving Mound Street its name)—simply known as South Columbus.

The sale of the first available lots in Columbus began on June 18, 1812, centered mostly on land around Broad and High Streets. They sold for two hundred to a thousand dollars, and the sale was over in three days. June 18, 1812, was also the first day of the War of 1812, often called the Second American Revolution. Only this time, not only were the United States and

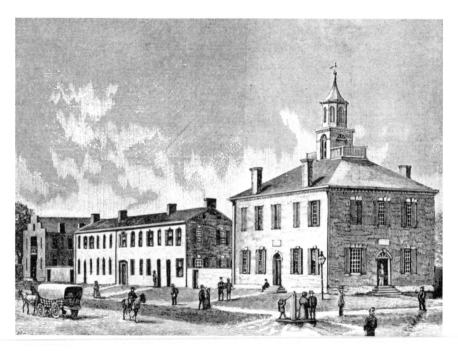

An 1846 drawing of the first Ohio Statehouse, used from 1816 to 1852. Taverns and saloons grew around this government center. *CML.*

Great Britain involved in the conflict, but also the Native American tribes in Ohio, many of whom lived in and near Franklinton and Columbus.

Of the first twelve lots purchased in 1812, two were acquired by Germans. Christian Heyl, one of the purchasers, connected several cabins on High Street near Rich and built a bakery and a house of entertainment. A bakery and a tavern might seem like an odd combination, but the bakery marked a new phase in Columbus's growth—the beginnings of a commercial venture for bread, an item once baked only at home. Within six years, Heyl erected the front of his tavern building. The building improvements were marked by a new name for the establishment, now called the Franklin House. It later became the Nagle House for over twenty years.

This architectural evolution is noteworthy. Heyl's tavern and bakery had been a log construction, probably with wooden pegs, as no nail manufacturers were established in Columbus at the time and nails were expensive. By connecting several cabins together, Heyl had created added retail and probably inn space. Later, he fronted the building with a sided façade that suggests both stability and room for signage. The next step in tavern architectural evolution would be from log and frame buildings to two-story brick structures.

President James Monroe and his entourage passed through Columbus in August 1817, while returning to Washington from Detroit following an inspection of public fortifications in the west. He was met in Worthington and escorted to Columbus for a major reception at the first Statehouse (not the present Statehouse), on the corner of State and South High Streets, conveniently located near several drinking establishments.

Wearing an old-fashioned, three-cornered, cocked hat (considered old fashioned in 1817) and plain clothing, and showing a perpetually sunburned face, Monroe complimented "the infant city," as he called Columbus, and its citizens. The visit was remembered forty years later by those who witnessed it. In the same year, William Lusk began a series of almanacs and noted that in Franklinton, still the county seat at this time, was a post office, a store, three taverns, a common school and an academy. The academy taught grammar, geography, trigonometry, navigation, astronomy, bookkeeping and two types of surveying, and it should be noted that Mr. Lusk also ran the school.

This was the era of a young nation trying to establish its own sense of place, mythologies and connections to its European heritages. It is no accident that Ohio has a Vienna, a Warsaw, a Paris, a London, a Lima, a Toledo, a Berlin and the like, nor is it unusual that taverns' names sounded very British, with lions or swans. Likewise, children were often named for historical, biblical or mythological figures or American heroes. Columbus names like Fernando Cortez (Fernando Cortez Kelton), George Washington (George Washington Beers), and Apollo (Apollo Maynard) were not odd. After all, Parson Weems was making up stories about the young George Washington chopping down cherry trees. What seems odd is that no one named his child Christopher Columbus.

That the "infant city" bore the name "Columbus" did not figure prominently in tavern marketing except in a few cases. No chamber of commerce was sitting around a tavern table, suddenly patting themselves on the back for their clever wordplay—"Discover Columbus."

Jeremiah Armstrong was twenty-seven years old when he purchased a High Street lot for the purpose of starting a "respectable hotel" in 1813. Armstrong's hotel was called the Christopher Columbus, with a full-sized sign of the city's namesake, but it was later changed to the Red Lion, perhaps because it was safer to harken back to the English grog shop.

Armstrong was no stranger to Columbus, having grown up in Franklinton, but his early childhood had been marred by a horrific and tragic experience that must have been told and retold in many Columbus taverns. Few stories could have been more galvanizing than the story this innkeeper told about his own life.

Armstrong had lived in Virginia near the Ohio River as a child with his parents and younger siblings. His mother had premonitions that she would suffer the same fate as her parents who had been killed by Native Americans, and indeed, Armstrong's life would be affected by his mother's fears.

When Armstrong was nine years old, he remembered seeing his mother for the last time, holding a candle in the night for his father as he went to check a trotline in the Ohio River. She was, in his words, trembling "like a leaf," so much so that the candle shook in her hand, and young Armstrong suspected she feared Indians because that seemed to be the only fear she had.

Decades later, in 1858, William Martin, early chronicler of Franklinton and Columbus history, recorded the story from the then-retired innkeeper. Imagine hearing the tale by firelight in the Red Lion:

In the middle of the night, the family was awakened by their dog's barking, and the father…

> spr[a]ng up, and without waiting to put on any clothing unbarred one of
> the doors, and ran out and hissed the dog; but in a moment he saw several
> Indians start from behind the trees, hallooed 'Indians,' and ran back into

A number of Franklinton residents had experienced captivity by Native Americans. Their stories were very much like this one shown in the 1760s, depicting Colonel Bouquet negotiating for prisoner return. *CML.*

the house, barred the door, and caught up a gun. By this time, the house was surrounded by twenty Wyandots. The poor, faithful dog had kept them off till he was disabled; they had cut him so badly in the mouth that his under jaw hung loose.

As the savages approached the house, father fired the gun; then caught a bullet pouch, and sprang to the loft, put his bullet and powder into his hand, but in attempting to put it into the gun found (too late) that he had taken the wrong pouch, and the bullet was too large; so he threw down the gun, tore open the roof, and sprang to the ground, fully expecting to be tomahawked the instant he reached it; but fortunately he was not discovered, for the most of the Indians were already in the house. They commenced their bloody work by killing the three little ones. Mother attempted to escape through the chimney, but it is supposed that her clothes caught, for she fell and (as the Indians afterward told me) in attempting to raise her they found she could not stand;

her hip was broken. Had she been able to travel, they would have not killed her; but as she could not, they must have her scalp as a trophy. They also scalped the two oldest of the children, but from my mother they took two.

They dry these scalps on little hoops, about the size of a dollar, paint them, and fix them on poles, to raise as trophies of victory when entering their villages. When seeing these so raised, I inquired why they took two from mother? They said because the babe's hair was not long enough to scalp, they took one from its mother for it. After killing my sisters and brother below, they came up to us and took us down. Oh! Who can describe our feelings on entering that room of blood! I was led over the slippery, bloody floor, and placed between the knees of one of the savages, whose hands were still reeking with the blood of my dearest relatives.

Mr. Misner, who lived about a hundred yards above us, hearing the noise, took a canoe and started for Belpre to raise an alarm. When half way across the river, I suppose, he saw the Indians and my sister; she was standing in the door and the house was lighted.

Mr. M. called, "What is the matter?"

One of the Indians told her to say nothing, which she did, being afraid to disobey. After plundering the house, they, with their three prisoners, started south-west; they went rapidly for a mile or two, then halted, formed a ring around us, and lighted their pipes, and made several speeches, apparently in great haste. We watched their gestures and listened anxiously. I was afterward told that I was the subject of their debate. They expected to be pursued by the people of Belpre, and thought me too young to travel as fast as necessary for their safety; so they proposed killing me; but a young Indian who had observed my activity in jumping the logs, said he thought I would make a pretty good Indian, and they might go as fast as they pleased, and if I could not keep up, he would carry me.

Armstrong and his brother, John, eventually were reunited with an older brother, William, but not before Armstrong had become thoroughly assimilated and attached to his adopted family. His sister, who had been taken by another tribe, was kidnapped out of captivity near Detroit by a man looking for his own sister who had been kidnapped.

After the signing of the Treaty of Greenville, in which most of Ohio was ceded to whites, the tribes were obligated to give up all prisoners. However, Armstrong and his brother refused to leave the old chief and their adopted families, and William Armstrong, their older brother, was forced to drag them off with the help of other men.

The Capital City's Most Storied Saloons

They succeeded in getting us into the boat and pushing off, leaving the old squaw who had the care of me, standing on the bank crying. There she stood, and I could hear her cries until lost in the distance. I cried too, till quite exhausted, and I fell asleep...some days after we started, William related the story of our capture, the murder of our mother, sisters and brother...Oh, what a change it wrought in me. It brought back the whole scene so forcibly to my recollection that I clung to my brother with affection and gratitude.

These were scary times to be living on the western edge of the war. Armstrong's story had happened only sixteen years before the town was founded and must have been told in many Columbus taverns to newcomers.

In 1812, Columbus was actually more Southern than Northern, settled by Virginians and Kentuckians whose native states had been dotted with distilleries and bourbons. It is reported that mint juleps were sipped here. Even if there were many Presbyterians and Calvinists among the early arrivals, Columbus was no dry town.

If the frontier generation was growing older and there were few men of Armstrong's age left to tell firsthand stories of respecting and fearing the Wyandots and Shawnes, the next generation was crafting its own tales about its favorite sports. One sport was politics, mainly the happenings of the Whig party, and the other—perhaps in lieu of the professional sports teams that would not appear for decades, Columbus's first favorite sport—land and its development, real estate, and speculative ventures. Where better to talk about real estate and land? To obtain information or launch a few hints of one's own? In a tavern, of course.

While small one-story log and frame stores in Columbus were the norm, there was one small brick building belonging to the Worthington Manufacturing Company that sold merchandise. With the stores established, taverns quickly came next.

Historic sources say that neither Heyl's nor Armstrong's taverns were the first. Columbus's first tavern was said to have been opened by Volney Payne in the spring of 1813. Perhaps his Lion and Eagle Tavern was the first Columbus tavern in a two-story brick dwelling erected for the purpose of being a tavern.

John Colett, the builder, may have had the building completed as a speculative venture, looking for a tenant willing to open a tavern. The Lion and Eagle later became the Globe under another owner. Columbus historian Ed Lentz has noted that the new owner, Robert Russell, had a

Pictured is C.M. Hubbard Hay Baler and Swan Tavern (built in 1816 and demolished in 1912), as seen in 1901. *CML.*

flare for gimmicks. Most might think a game of darts or duckpins would be a novelty. Not Mr. Russell. He brought in a circus, theater performances and even a performing bear to attract customers. The tavern lasted until the 1840s, but it would not be the only bear attraction in Columbus taverns.

As soon as Mr. Payne opened his tavern, Daniel Kooser opened another on Front Street, south of State Street. Then another tavern opened on Front Street, north of Broad Street, owned by Mr. McCollum. These were followed by another tavern and another tavern and another tavern.

Both Payne's and McCollum's taverns—known as houses of entertainment where little else other than drinking and possibly gaming went on—and more upscale or "respectable" inns or hotels appeared almost simultaneously. They sprang up like mushrooms at the intersections of dirt roads—at the northeast corner of High and Rich Streets, the southeast corner of High and Town Streets and on Friend Street (Livingston Avenue) just west of High Street.

William Day owned a house of entertainment near Town and Rich Streets in 1815–1816 that acquired a reputation for hard drinking and serious quarreling. It earned the nickname of the "War Office." When the combat turned physical among the drinkers, the miscreants were taken to Squire Shields, a Justice of the Peace, to be disposed of according to the law.

As described by nineteenth-century historian William Martin, Shields was "a rather eccentric old genius from the Emerald Isle" who could dispose of business in short order. He was an expeditious man, whether he was applying the law or doing one of his many other occupations—Methodist preacher, bricklayer and surveyor—and he was famous for keeping his temper even under volatile circumstances. William Martin related:

> *On one occasion, when in his office, one of his rough customers very abruptly called him a liar, to which the 'Squire coolly replied in his broad Irish brogue: "Poh, man, we are all liars—I can prove you a liar!" at which the other bristled up as though he was for fight—*
>
> *"Prove me a liar! prove me a liar! Can you?"*
>
> *The 'Squire making no further reply, turned to a file of notes that had been sued before him, and picking out one of his hero's notes and presenting the name to him, asked if that was his signature? To which the man replied "Yes; and what of it?"*
>
> *The 'Squire reads: "Three months after date, I promise to pay," etc, "and did you pay?"*
>
> *"I will pay when I am ready!" was the reply.*
>
> *"There, Sir," said the 'Squire, "I have proved you a liar under your own hand;" and returning the note to its place, without further ado, sat down to his writing.*

David Broderick, who had owned a Franklinton tavern, opened a "respectable" tavern in 1815 at the corner of Town and High Streets, naming the establishment the Columbus Inn. It was not a log structure but a frame building. It is reported that the first regular meetings of city council were held here in 1816, and the tavern lasted until the 1830s.

In the same year (1815), James Gardiner opened his tavern. His respectable tavern was on Friend Street, west of High Street. When Mr. Broderick retired three years later, Gardiner took over the tavern at Town and High Streets, under the new colorful name the Rose Tree, adding the quotation from the Bible, "The wilderness shall blossom as the rose," as part of the sign. Gardiner's business on Friend Street was taken over by Jarvis Pike, a mayor of Columbus, and he renamed it the Yankee Tavern.

History does not record who opened the "less respectable" taverns. Warning! If it seems one needs a play book to keep track of all these addresses and name changes, there will be bad news and good news as the story goes on. The bad news is that there will be many more taverns and saloons to keep track of. The good news is that every other building seems to be a tavern or saloon, and it won't matter.

Toasting and land speculation were nightly drinking companions at the National Hotel, run by John Noble; the Globe Hotel, owned by Robert Russell; the Grover Boarding House; the Farmers and Mechanics' Tavern; and a number of places named for a variety of animals generally not seen in Columbus—the Red Lion (Jerimiah Armstrong); the Swan Tavern, also called Swan Hotel, (Christian Heyl); the Eagle Hotel (David Brooks); and the White Horse (Amos Meneely). They were all in close proximity—of course, the town was only a few blocks wide and a few blocks long, and still very much a wilderness as illustrated by the Great Squirrel Hunt of 1822 in which the men of the city killed 19,866 annoying squirrels in one day.

In one historical account, the White Horse was best described as "a wagon yard," though this may not mean people were just sitting around drinking among the wagons, but rather refers to a location. It would be hard to think that there was no structure, since at one point, one of the owners was a very respectable lady, Keziah Hamlin, who as a child lived

Keziah Hamlin Brooks (1804–1875), captured by Indians as a child, was the first white woman born in Columbus and co-owner of the White Horse Tavern. *CML.*

with her parents in the first cabin built on the east side of the Scioto. She, too, must have related her own story in the White Horse.

The Wyandots were very fond of her mother's freshly baked bread and occasionally helped themselves to it without asking, though they left venison or other game behind in exchange. One day, as Mrs. Hamlin was busy, they came into the cabin and silently took her sleeping infant. Fearful of what might happen to her child, Mrs. Hamlin grew more agitated as the hours went by, but she was relieved to see the Wyandots return at the end of the day with Keziah in their arms. On Keziah's feet was a pair of beaded moccasins, perfectly fitted. Keziah later married David Brooks and had five children, one of whom became a well-known Columbus banker. Sadly, the moccasins were accidentally destroyed, but the story has remained.

Officially, Columbus was incorporated as a city in February 1834, having achieved the necessary required population. In addition to having federal officials of the courts (an attorney, marshal, clerk, postmaster, superintendent of the National Road and even an Indian agent), Columbus had nine state officials; eleven practicing physicians; twenty-two dry goods and grocery sellers; two booksellers; a number of leather stores; some scattered comb, broom and hat factories; and nine "official" taverns—one less than the ten practicing attorneys, but one more than the eight officiating clergymen. Of the eight Columbus clergymen, four were Methodists and one was an agent for a temperance society. Unofficially, there were many more places to buy a drink.

In the 1830s and 1840s, refreshment and gaming were available at the Eagle Coffee House across High Street from the first Statehouse, located approximately at 63 or 69 South High, according to the late Columbus historian and *Citizen-Journal* columnist Ben Hayes. Coffee and chocolate houses had been in America for over a hundred years and were popular in Boston and New York City, and they were considered more refined than taverns.

A coffeehouse was where proper gentlemen could meet, and both food and liquor were served. Forty years before the Eagle Coffeehouse appeared in Columbus, a New York City coffeehouse, the Tontine Coffee House at Wall and Water Streets, was well established and elegant. It shared space with the stock exchange and insurance offices, where every ship's arrival and departure was noted. Set up as a private club, the Tontine also had indoor privies, baths, a tearoom and a dining room with mahogany furniture and crystal chandeliers.

Of course, New York City had a lot of things that Columbus did not have at the time—like free-standing eating houses (restaurants) to serve the many

Snyder Chaffee Chocolate Shop at 47 North High Street, circa 1890s. Early chocolate shops were seen as rivals to coffee houses that served liquor. *CML.*

workers who wolfed down food or New York City's Bank Coffee House where the gimmick was to wheel in a whole standing bear, fully cooked and ready to slice and serve.

But wait.

To be fair, Columbus's Eagle Coffee House also had a bath and a bear— of course, it was one and the same. The tavern had a public bathhouse with water stored in an underground cistern and a large black bear tethered to a treadmill. Operating the treadmill with its feet, the bear pumped water to create a shower. As inhumane as it might sound to tether a bear, the bear at the Bank Coffee House, fully cooked and served whole, certainly fared worse. At least, Columbus's working bear periodically escaped, chased the patrons and probably enjoyed creating a little panic in the streets.

The Eagle Coffee House became famous on April 9, 1840, when it was favored by the Whigs as their meeting place to organize the Franklin County Tippecanoe Club. Here they pledged support for General William Harrison for president of the United States ("Tippecanoe and Tyler Too"). On this occasion, it was said that the proprietor of the Eagle had, "with kindness and foresight," supplied a barrel of hard cider for the refreshment of those gathered. While the supporters drank the cider from a gourd, they admired a miniature "Fort Meigs" brought by the Wood County delegation. The miniature structure sported two flags, the Stars and Stripes and a Bird of

Liberty, and was used as a rostrum for the speakers. The Tippecanoe Club was a powerful political organization for many years.

While the Eagle Coffee House was popular with lawyers and Whigs, the Democrats often held impromptu caucus sessions at a rival tavern, the Tontine, near the statehouse. Notice Columbus was not about to be undone by New York, and both shared using the name Tontine Coffee House. Although, as historian Alfred Lee noted, "Among the exhilarating drinks dispensed…coffee was one of the last called for, or thought of."

Anyone who was important, especially leaders of the Whig party, came by the coffeehouse, except the Reverend James Hoge, a Presbyterian pillar of learning and decorum. The Eagle was eventually sold, becoming the Commercial, and by 1876, hardware merchant and developer E.T. Mithoff acquired the property for development. He had the old building torn down—presumably the bear had passed on long before. Mithoff believed that High Street property was becoming too increasingly valuable for the likes of an old tavern to remain.

The unhealthy water in Columbus made alcohol a health-food drink. Typhoid and cholera, two water-born, deadly diseases described in the next

An 1888 drawing of the Scioto River's east bank, extending from the State Street Bridge to the Town Street Bridge. *CML.*

chapter, were bred in foul ditches. Of course, the biggest ditch of all was the feeder canal that connected Columbus and the Ohio Erie Canal system, stretching from Lake Erie to the Ohio River. Though no one could have known that a major cholera epidemic was still years away, it was easier to tackle another epidemic—nightly roustabouts and drunks.

In 1828, an ordinance was passed to curb intoxicated evildoers who might be strolling about after 10:00 p.m., and one year later, an ordinance included intoxicated people in the same category as vagrants, idlers or lewd people who might be disorderly or riotous. The need for the two ordinances shows Columbus's exciting nightlife following a few drinks.

The work on the feeder canal started with ceremony, parades and a trip to Christian Heyl's tavern. Columbus's economy was as stagnant as much of the water, and four years of building a ditch eleven miles long, four feet deep and forty feet wide would be spent to connect Columbus's Main Street to Lockbourne, Ohio. The canal was completed in 1831, built by Irish unskilled labor and Ohio Penitentiary prisoners. In two months after opening, the canal brought new merchandise and goods to Columbus and, more importantly, new people. It also created a need for warehouses along the river and a need for taverns and boardinghouses.

Stagecoaches left Columbus daily for Springfield and Cincinnati, Mount Vernon and Cleveland, and Chillicothe and Wheeling. The frontier taverns

The feeder canal was built in 1831 by unskilled Irish labor and Ohio Penitentiary prisoners. *CML.*

and inns began to evolve into another generation of establishments—the hotel with a tavern, more refined and more suitable to meeting the growing needs of the many travelers who came by way of canal, National Road and railroads. A hotel generally could boast having a dining room, although it frequently served food and drink in a regimentation that annoyed European travelers. The "American Plan" charged for room and food in one fee regardless if the meal was missed or ignored. In Columbus, according to historian Paton Yoder, boarders were summoned to meals by a gong or bell from outside the hotel. In Columbus, it seemed punctuality was important and a "sort of competition" existed among the hotels as to which establishment could ring the loudest and longest bell and which could add a warning bell.

The hotels could become so crowded that families continued to take in guests. Those seeking a room were often lawyers or drovers, but the majority was "movers," those moving to new lands. Lydia Rose McCabe, a young Columbus journalist whose remembrances are well documented in her book *Don't You Remember?*, recalled her 1830s trip on the canal boat as a mirthful journey of talk and laughter among fellow passengers, including a major and veteran of the 1812 War, an Englishman, a lawyer and two Irishmen who each boasted about whose ancestor arrived first in America. They stopped

An early example of stagecoaches that would have arrived in Columbus is the Bullitt Park Stagecoach, as seen in 1891. *CML.*

at the National Hotel, a tavern, where Henry Clay was once entertained and where he was treated to a new delicacy: meringue.

The National Hotel was the site of parties during the legislative sessions, hosted by a beautiful Southern woman whose first husband was a jealous and murdering Spaniard. Now married to her cousin, a Democratic legislator, she was a much talked about patron of parties. When the Ohio legislature was in session, the party and theater season was in full swing. Some of the 1820s ordinances against riotous and lewd alcoholic behavior were modified or ignored so that tavern owners and innkeepers did not lose money and so that legislative sessions could continue the next day. Billiards and roulette were popular, but there were also gambling ordinances in place. These too were not enforced when the legislature was in session.

New hotels—each with their famed dining rooms, gathering spots and watering holes—emerged in the young state capital. The American House, built in 1834, stood at State and High Streets (the present site of the Vern Riffe Center). The Buckeye House stood across the street from the Ohio Statehouse (present site of James Rhodes Office Tower). Hotel rooms were hard to come by during busy times, and even respectable people, like Samuel

Pictured is East Broad Street, across from the statehouse, as seen in 1889. In addition to the Hayden Clinton Bank Building and the imposing Board of Trade Building is the Buckeye House, another famous early hotel. *CML.*

Chase, later with President Lincoln's cabinet, had to share a room and the only bed with a stranger. When the capital was especially crowded, men who shared rooms at the American House often slept two to the bed and four or five on the floor, wagon wheel–style, meaning they slept with their heads in the center and their smelly feet on the outside.

There was probably only one hotel in town where liquor was not served—the Temperance Hotel.

The Neil House, which had three reincarnations with the third lasting into the twentieth century, started as a log cabin tavern across from the Statehouse by William Neil in 1818. Neil had made his fortunes in the stagecoach business, in lucrative contracts with the Ohio legislature for the improvements (which many claimed were never improved) of the Worthington-Sandusky Plank Road (High Street) that ran past his farm in North Columbus, and in Columbus's favorite sport, real estate and land speculation. Neil owned all the land north of Fifth Avenue stretching to Lane Avenue. What he did not own, his son Robert owned, including Neil's Woods, where Fort Hayes stands today.

The second Neil House Hotel, across from the statehouse, as seen in this 1901 photo. It opened in 1862 and was replaced with a third Neil House in 1923, which remained until 1980. *CML.*

To capture the sense of an early Columbus tavern and inn, one might journey to the Worthington Inn, ten miles north of downtown Columbus; Lafayette's Red Brick Tavern; Lebanon's Golden Lamb; or Columbus's Jury Room.

For many years, it was believed that the present-day Jury Room, which bares a resemblance to the Red Brick Tavern, was built in the 1850s by Thomas Asbury, a veteran of the American Revolution, and later sold by Ashbury and his wife, Sarah, to Jacob Fahrbach in 1864. It was also thought that the building was completely destroyed and rebuilt after a fire about 1870.

Court house records lost in frequent fires, early city directories with no street locations and no references to owners, drinking establishments with no names and modern county auditor's sites that list properties as "old" have not been helpful. By the 1870s, the building appears as the J.F. Gaiser Saloon and Boarding House and is easier to track.

However, the building is clearly older in its simple style, use of materials, basement and foundation walls. Early maps, fragments of records, relative location to other known establishments, detective work by previous local historians and covered-over charred ceiling beams seem to indicate that the building is from the 1830s. At times, it is hard to determine if it was a house first and then a tavern or if the two purposes co-mingled. Being on Mound Street but pulled back from the intersection at South High Street, the Jury

Pictured in 1876, the three-story J.F. Gaiser Saloon and Boarding House suffered a fire, losing most of the top floor and was rebuilt. It still exists today as the Jury Room. *CD.*

Room is certainly in the right place at the right time to have survived. The building, whatever its name was, would have been around to welcome the coming of the canal.

The feeder canal's groundbreaking was in 1827, and the mayor and 899 of his closest friends would have marched down the slope of the present-day Mound Street to the river. They marched with shovels and wheelbarrows and dumped the first loads of excavated earth to the side in a symbolic gesture—and left the real work of the next four years to others. By then, the Jury Room building would have been there.

During that same time period, the towns of Lockbourne and Reynoldsburg were laid out. Famed writer Alexander DeTocqueville started his tour across America, Andrew Jackson was running for president and Nat Turner's rebellion was terrorizing the South. Columbus had 350 dwellings and ten lawyers, and the commodities most often advertised in the newspapers were whiskey, salt petre, turpentine, indigo and vanilla cream candy.

The original Franklin County courthouse was still on the west side of the Scioto in Franklinton, but the land at Capitol Square had been graded for improvements. The Jury Room's neighbor across the street (the southeast corner of Mound and High Streets) was an unusually large Indian mound,

The cornerstone laying of the Franklin County Courthouse in 1885. The Jury Room is pictured in the background (second building from left). *CML.*

large enough to have a house and homoeopathic doctor's office on top of it. Eventually the mound was taken down. Its clay was made up of generations of river gravel that made good bricks and became part of the original Statehouse at State and Broad.

In the 1840s, the building's neighbors were blacksmiths, tailors, shoemakers, stonecutters, millers, saddlers and pump dealers. The city's population had about more than doubled to about 5,500 of whom 600 were African Americans. There were now nineteen churches, three schools, four banks, four fire engine companies, eight Masonic or Odd Fellow fraternal lodes, a "musical saloon" and five temperance societies working in opposition to the three hundred saloons in the city. It is unclear what a musical saloon was. By the late nineteenth century, the term was used to mean a tavern with dancing girls who distracted patrons so the patrons' pockets could be picked. Dancing girls in the 1840s sounds unlikely, but then again…

For many years, the Jury Room building did not have a specific name, though its downstairs was a tavern and its upstairs was sometimes used as sleeping quarters for either the families who ran the tavern or guests. The Jury Room flourished throughout the Civil War, but those stories are in the next chapter.

In the 1870s, after the war, John Gaiser owned the tavern and sometimes lived upstairs, although his home was also listed as being on Germania and Jaeger. The building and businesses have long been associated with the German community, and originally, the German community stretched north to Rich Street.

The saloon was conveniently located near a center of barristers and legal activity. Because of its proximity to the courthouses, the Jury Room has been considered the cradle of judges, and as evidenced by the stories from other early taverns, the cases have been tried, influenced or retried here.

In 1879, following a disastrous courthouse fire that destroyed many public records, a new building campaign was on to create the new courthouse. The Franklin County Courthouse cornerstone was laid on July 4, 1885, and early photos show the Jury Room building standing at 22 East Mound.

Designed by George Bellows, father of the famous Ashcan artist of the same name, the courthouse was an imposing French Second Empire style. By 1885, the establishment was called Wine and Beer Saloon and Boarding House, but it was owned by both Gaiser and his brother, Fred. An advertising signboard found in the basement may confirm this name. Railroaders used the boardinghouse when they worked in town, and the lively activities during the Civil War may have continued.

The Jury Room, located since 1831 at 22 East Mound Street. *TB.*

Street photo of the Jury Room as seen today. Its size and scale was typical of early nineteenth-century taverns. *TB.*

For all its convenience in location, the Wine and Beer Saloon must have had fierce competition. In 1888, there were more than 440 saloons from Livingston Avenue to the Union Station, the Scioto River to Washington Boulevard. Four hundred and forty saloons in a city with nineteen banks, thirteen billiard parlors, twelve Chinese laundries, 190 doctors and 117 meat sellers. There were probably more saloons that did not have names, or perhaps even licenses.

The Jury Room was later owned by Peter Weirich and his son in 1894 and bore the name Weirich and Son. They lived at 196 East Beck. John Weirich, presumably a relative who ran the establishment, lived on the property upstairs or in back. Weinrich and Son was located next to an Independent German Protestant church (whose minister lived in the rectory that later became the Maennerchor building on South High Street). In addition to the Franklin County courthouse across the street, there were dry goods stores, apartments, a Chinese Merchants Association, boardinghouses and…other saloons.

The building at 22 East Mound is significant because its history spans many eras and many themes—it is a rare remaining oddity in a city often accused of "tear down and move-on." In its first one hundred years, it is the inn and tavern emerging from the frontier and the German immigrant experience. In the chapters ahead, the Jury Room's connection to the sectarian differences of Civil War Columbus, the almost exclusively men's world of politics and public affairs and the temperance and anti-saloon movement's answer to social excesses will be told.

Chapter 2

Little Germany and
Irish Broadway

Drink and Romanticism in the Age of Typhoid

*For the most part, in the first century after the Declaration of Independence
immigrants were from the most civilized nations of Europe, and were
seeking liberty and land for homes. Now, however, an increasing number
of them come or are brought from the less enlightened European nations
and from heathen countries, seeking simply better wages, and caring little
or nothing for land or homes. They are sadly lacking in education and
religion, and are by no means well fitted for the citizenship of a republic.*
—Lucy Hayes (Mrs. Rutherford Hayes), diary, 2 April 1881

*No wonder that those Irish lads
Should be so gay and frisky,
For sure St. Pat he taught them that,
As well as making whiskey...*
—Henry Bennett, Irish author and performer, 1890

*Henry B. Hunter,
165 South High, between Town & Rich Sts.,
West Side, Columbus, Ohio,
Dealer in Drugs, Medicines, Chemicals, Fine Toilet Soaps, Fine Hair and
Tooth Brushes, Perfumery, Pure Wines and Liquors for Medicinal Uses,
Fancy and Toilet Articles, Trusses & Shoulder Braces, Tobacco, Cigars, Etc.*
—from an advertisement in Martin's History of Franklin County, 1858

L et's face it. Taverns, saloons and drinking were part of nineteenth-century Columbus life for a number of reasons. For one thing, it was a cultural practice among the Germans, Irish and others who arrived in numbers. For another, no one really wanted to drink water.

Mrs. Rutherford B. Hayes, also known as Lemonade Lucy for her temperance views and prohibition of alcohol in the White House, clearly saw the new immigrants as unworthy of citizenship. The Irish made whiskey, although it is doubtful that a thirteenth-century saint taught them this art. The Germans made beer, and stores sold alcohol for medicinal purposes to ease the fever, miasma and ague that plagued Columbus, in addition to the expected illnesses or complications of injury, childbirth or tuberculosis. None, however, were so dreaded as typhoid or cholera.

River water was probably not what most citizens of Columbus wanted to drink. Columbus relied on the artesian wells for clean water, water bubbling naturally from underground water tables from fissures in rock. Throughout the nineteenth century, on the east side of the Scioto and Olentangy Rivers, there

Pictured in 1908, the Scioto River was already flowing with industrial waste and sewage. *CML.*

were numerous streams that flowed into the Scioto. In addition, Columbus had numerous ponds, marshes, bogs and swamps. The bog near the intersection of State Street and Grant Avenue was known as Frog Heaven. Every spring, hoards of peepers turned into noisy croakers, keeping residents awake.

Artesian wells once created natural springs, like Mirror Lake at the Ohio State University, and provided clean water for the William Neil family whose house sat where the Main Library is today. According to university records, the water of Mirror Lake was one of the reasons the university's trustees chose this spot for the Ohio Agricultural and Mechanical College and why people came from across the city to collect water, until a mishap occurred when a sewer system was being installed and construction punctured a main artery. The water dried up in the 1880s. William Neil's sons, Robert and Henry, built their mansion at Fifteenth and Indianola Avenues near the spring that flowed through the Iuka Ravine.

Spring Street was so named because a natural spring, Doe Run (now encased in century-old brick vaults through downtown), ran to the river. John Deshler, whose grandparents, David and Betsy, owned the northwest corner of Broad and High Streets, remembered in the 1900s that the spring was teeming with fish after heavy rains. The many ravines were created by such runoffs, and water tables were filled after spring rains. Peter's Run (now under I-70 through downtown) once fed clean water into the breweries of Little Germany.

But many people realized that the rivers were not appealing, though the connection between contaminated water and disease was not fully realized, before the mid-nineteenth century and disease control in Great Britain. Early advertisements boasted that ice was cut two miles above downtown—as if no one three miles or more upstream was dumping anything foul into the river. Ice cut in winter was stored in icehouses and sold in summer. Children would run after ice wagons in the hopes of getting slivers of ice to suck on hot days. Imagine a slushy made of Scioto River water.

Early Columbus occasionally suffered from typhoid fever, caused by the *Salmonella typhi* bacteria found in contaminated food or water and carried by human waste. The bacteria can survive for weeks in dried sewage and has a fatality rate of about 20 percent.

Though typhoid had always been recurrent in Columbus throughout the nineteenth century, an unprecedented epidemic of typhoid fever occurred in the late 1880s.

This time, an outside expert, Allen Hazen of New York, and a separate group investigated the Columbus water supply. They agreed—it was the water. The mayor and others reached a gentlemen's agreement that an

Dirty water continued to spread typhoid and cholera into the early twentieth century, as pictured here in 1908. *CML.*

impounding dam in the Scioto River would be built, but the recommended purification plant would be built later when more funds were available and voters agreed to the expense. However, the leading doctors of the day in Columbus—Dr. Starling Loving, Dr. J.F. Baldwin, Dr. E.B. Fullerton and Dr. Will Hamilton—spoke out against the unnecessary expenses since, they believed, no system of water purification could remove the germs of typhoid fever. As old-school doctors of the previous generation, they had little education in sanitary conditions.

By the late nineteenth century, specific complaints about Columbus's water focused on the many streams and the ravine water that ran into the rivers. In addition to industrial and human waste, local slaughterhouses contributed sewage and offal. However, these complaints were classified as nuisance abatement, and boards of health felt it was not within their authority to address these complaints. Despite an 1897 law that allowed the Ohio State Board of Health to study the streams of Ohio as sources of water supply for public use and an 1898 Columbus law that established a city laboratory to conduct bacteriological examinations, the government was reluctant to offer an immediate remedy to Columbus's water problem.

The Capital City's Most Storied Saloons

A 1903 advertisement from Anheuser-Busch Brewing Association in St. Louis was published in the *Columbus Citizen* newspaper. It claimed:

> *Pure Water is better than poor beer. Pure beer is more wholesome than pure water because of the nourishing qualities of malt and the tonic properties of hops. Budweiser is brewed from malt made under our own supervision, the finest hops available, and thoroughly filtered soft river water (—river water contains no mineral salts and is therefore best adapted for the production of good beers—), thus making it the Essence of Purity. No household is complete without this nourishing, refreshing table beverage, the "King of Bottled Beers."*

While Anheuser-Busch might not have done itself any favors in mentioning the use of river water, the safer substitute for water, in the minds of many, was alcohol, especially beer. It is no accident that an age of typhoid and cholera in urban areas was also the golden age of taverns and saloons.

By 1903, the citizens of Columbus, being better informed of sanitation issues, passed a bond levy to improve the city's sewage system and purification

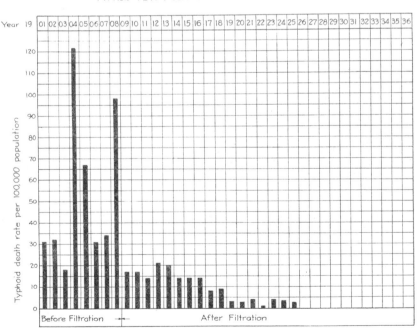

Within the first quarter of the twentieth century, cases of typhoid dropped dramatically with improved sanitation. *CML.*

of its sewage. Typhoid fever, like tuberculosis, was a recurrent threat and cause of death, but it did not produce the public panic of cholera, sometimes called "King Cholera" because both rich and poor were its subjects.

Cholera is a waterborne disease caused by bacteria that leave a toxin in the small intestines. It is found in water carrying fecal material, in public wells or on vegetables or fruit contaminated by such water. It can lay dormant for long periods, but when the cholera bacteria, *Vibrio cholerae*, enters the human body, severe dehydration occurs, and a victim can lose a quart of body fluids an hour—death can occur in a few hours after the onset of the disease. In epidemics, the death rate can be as high as 90 percent.

A worldwide cholera epidemic reached the United States in the 1830s, and Columbus specifically was in the midst of an epidemic in 1833, recurring many more times. The 1833 epidemic was traced to a pandemic that originated in Bengal, India, in 1817, spreading through Russia, Europe, Great Britain and Ireland. Cholera followed the commerce, migration, immigration and transportation networks. Immigrants, especially, were thought to carry cholera, and there may have been some reason to believe this, since ocean-going vessels discharged their bilge water close to ports, infecting anyone in contact with the shore.

In Columbus, cholera spread through open ditches. In 1833, in the town of almost five thousand people, there was no sewage system and no water works. Patrolling hogs took the place of garbage collection. English actor Oscar Wilde, on a trip through America, said the stench of roaming hogs in American cities was so great it "causes granite eyes to weep."

Household water was drawn from wells. Waste was left in cesspools and ditches sunk that were close to wells. When a well became fouled, a new well was created close by. Rotting garbage clogged gutters and created stagnant pools. In the 1833 cholera epidemic, Columbus printer-turned-botanic physician Dr. Howard claimed he had a "cholera syrup" that would defend against the disease. However, he, along with his wife, a daughter, a son-in-law and two grandchildren, was not saved by drinking cholera syrup. His daughter, a vivacious girl of twenty, met her friends at South High and Main Streets at noon to draw water. She was stricken with cholera at 2:00 p.m. and died at 4:00 p.m.

Bed rest, warm water, opium, a full dose of calomel (a form of mercury which loosened the teeth and caused hair to fall out), bloodletting, purging, iced drinks, iced creams and malt liquors were recommended. In Great Britain in the 1830s, the cholera epidemic was followed by a new awareness of the necessity for sanitation and clean water. However, in Columbus in the 1830s, the cholera epidemic was followed by collecting statistics, a condemning of the use of cholera syrup and maintaining business as usual—meaning a trip to the tavern to ruminate about what had happened, followed by an elimination, near the well, of body waste from too many beers.

When cholera returned in 1849, Columbus newspapers made suggestions for sanitation improvements based on how the English had approached the matter—removing rotting animal and vegetable impurities on the ground, avoiding impure drinking water, burying cholera victims' clothing away from human habitation and so on. Someone must have forgotten to tell the slaughterhouses, however, because they were still dumping offal everywhere, manure piles clogged High Street between State and Town Streets, and human waste from the Lunatic Asylum (located at East Broad Street near Jefferson Avenue at the time) was being dumped and clogging the Scioto River near the feeder canal.

It might have been the Romantic Age, but there was nothing romantic about horse-drawn vehicle power. A healthy horse could produce between twenty and twenty-five pounds of manure in a day (not a pretty math word problem). Dumped into the streams and rivers, manure polluted the water, but left on the ground, it would be pounded gradually into dust (especially in dry spells) and become a fine dust that covered clothes, blew into eyes and nostrils and tainted food. Conditions were ripe for another disaster.

With the completion of the National Road through Columbus, the appearance of the railroads and the use of the canals, European cholera hitched a ride with the newly arriving Irish and German immigrants. Mortality was greater, especially on the South Side where the Germans lived, than in previous outbreaks. The combined population in the city and surrounding counties had been about seventeen thousand in 1833. One year later, sixteen thousand remained.

Cholera returned in 1850, went underground and reemerged in 1866 and 1873. The Columbus cholera epidemic of 1873 arrived by way of New Orleans.

Dr. Davis Halderman, a physician at the Ohio Penitentiary, analyzed the geography of Columbus and the affected areas of waste pools along the Scioto River as it curved through the city. He noted the low points of the city where railroads, foundries and industries were under construction and/or where there had been a lack of drainage. Cesspools were everywhere. It was not hard to spot the sewers; they opened along the river above the waterline, pouring out their contents. Columbus's system of sewers was intended for flooding and drainage but was used for sanitary purposes—or, in this case, unsanitary purposes. Halderman plotted the cholera deaths against potential

As seen in this photo, the proximity of the Ohio Penitentiary to the river was a serious sanitary issue. The Scioto River experienced major flooding well before the great 1913 flood. *CML.*

places of pollution—railroad bridges, factories, low areas along the Scioto, tenements and the Ohio Penitentiary, where the daily excrement of over a thousand men went from buckets in the cells to the river.

Over time, ravines had become more sewers leading to the Scioto and Olentangy Rivers, and downtown Columbus on both sides of the Scioto was the largest sewer of all, containing industrial pollutants, animal feces, dead animals, tanneries, garbage and human waste.

And if it seems hard to believe that the connection between sanitation and health would not have been more obvious, consider how easy it is to lose the big picture. When the Ohio Statehouse was completed during the Civil War, it had already been a thirty-year, off-again, on-again building project of convict labor. The statehouse had the novelty of indoor privies. They worked fine—and such a luxury! No outdoor privies dotting the statehouse grounds. Years passed before it was realized that the maladies suffered by people in the building (the so-called Statehouse Malaria) was an illness caused from waste building up in the walls. Yes, it seems the filth of the privies was not connected to another nineteenth-century novelty—sewers—and barrels and barrels, wagonload after wagonload, had to be removed from behind interior walls. Where did it go? Probably the river.

Germans, often blamed as the cause of disease, also supplied the alternative to bad water—the beer. To understand German immigration, it is important to remember that Germans were already in Columbus when the first lots of the borough went on sale in 1812. Two Germans were among the first eighteen buyers of the new capital's lots. These lots were not cheap, costing between $200 and $1,000, with one-fifth down and four easy payments. The lot on the northwest corner of Broad and High where John Deshler would later build the famous Deshler Hotel (present One Columbus) cost $1,000. The Germans who purchased lots did not come without resources. To put the economy in perspective, less than 50 percent of all men in Columbus even owned land, and 10 percent of the property owners in all of Ohio owned 33 percent of all the property.

The Germans and Irish were both present in early Columbus, though the majority of them would arrive in the 1840s through the 1860s in the classic "push-pull" patterns. They would be pulled to America for opportunities, but they would be pushed from Europe because of revolutions, political upheavals and, in the case of the Irish, potato blight and starvation. In numbers there is power, and the German population was so influential in Ohio that, even as early as 1816, the Germans lobbied the Ohio legislature to have all laws in Ohio printed in both English and German. Eventually,

Hayes' Saloon, 1405 Livingston Avenue, was in business from 1897 to 1922. This interior scene, circa 1910, is typical of Columbus's saloons. *CML.*

the lobbying efforts, led by Germans from Columbus and Cincinnati, were successful, and for almost seven decades, all Ohio legislation was bilingual. Public schools were permitted to teach all subjects and all grades in English or German.

While Columbus was still in its infancy in 1813, a well-known community member and German immigrant, as mentioned before, Christian Heyl, opened a bakery and tavern in a log cabin. Later, he became a judge and a city council member, and his enterprise was the gathering spot for entertainment and politics—a common tie for all to the new town—a place where the community experienced public events together.

On warm days, men sat outside of the tavern, drinking slowly. To the passersby, it might seem that this was just another leisurely day, but the men were actually indulging in a common Columbus tavern custom—waiting for someone to get up to get another beer. The thirstiest man was then obligated to buy a round of drinks for all his comrades. Toasting was already getting noticed in the East, where it was frowned upon by many as encouraging binge drinking. However, it did not stop Columbus men from toasting women passing by the tavern on warm days. This included early Franklinton and Columbus businessman and confirmed bachelor Lyne Starling, who sat outside the Eagle Coffee House almost daily.

Songs, some ribald and sometimes sung while lying on the bar; the clink of glasses in toasts; the hurrahs over billiards or cards; a friendly drink that led to many more; or a legal argument in court that was rehashed in the tavern by lubricated barristers led to a well-known saying—"He knew more law when drunk than any other lawyer knew when sober."

This sense of community may explain why the German tavern gatherings were so important, and it is a part of what the Germans did best—the Germans' over-the-top, extravagant public displays for the Fourth of July were a hallmark of all German communities. Columbus's contemporary celebration of the holiday, the largest in the Midwest, is rooted in the Columbus Germans' Fourth of July celebrations.

Parades to the statehouse, the reading of the Declaration of Independence, the Columbus artillery demonstrations, German marching regiments, the picnicking and toasting and even the close of the holiday, starting in the mid-nineteenth century at a beer garden, all marked the early Fourth of July celebrations. Though the Irish, the Welsh and the native-born from Virginia through New England all marked the date in some way, the Germans were the most extravagant. The Fourth of July was one holiday that was truly American—and most importantly, nonreligious—and therefore shared by all.

The Capital City's Most Storied Saloons

For a people who had come from Europe where there was no country of Germany, and would not be until late nineteenth century, the Germans' enthusiastic and extravagant celebration of a nation's birthday was like hosting a birthday party on steroids (or perhaps beer, to be exact).

That the Germans saw themselves as a more convivial people, apt to enjoy a good beer, is apparent in how they compared themselves to their neighbors. They had a variety of nicknames for the other settlers of Columbus. The Virginians were "pinchguts," meaning they were stingy to the core. The New England settlers were "cold dumplings," who lacked a sense of humor and took life too seriously.

To put the push-pull theory into perspective in Columbus, hard as it might be to imagine, perhaps, the first large waves of Germans and Irish were arriving just as the Wyandots were leaving.

A resident of Franklinton named Armstrong (no relation to Jeremiah Armstrong who owned the Red Lion) had been kidnapped by the Wyandots when he was child. Armstrong lived, married, raised sons and died among the tribe. His two sons, both educated and one admitted to the Ohio bar, followed the Wyandots west, probably in 1843 when three chiefs of the Wyandots came through Columbus to say goodbye to the governor. Under a treaty passed the year before, the Wyandots were the last tribe to leave Ohio, giving up their land in Upper Sandusky for lands in Missouri. There were beautiful speeches, newspaper accounts of their journey by land and boat, a rush to buy land in Upper Sandusky and little remembrance in the legislature that the Wyandots were to receive payments.

No wonder that after James Fennimore Cooper's *Last of the Mohicans* had been translated into German, it became the most widely read book after German advice books for immigrants coming to America. It is no coincidence that German-speaking enclaves in America named places in respect for what they saw as the passing of a people who also no longer had a homeland of their own.

Beer flowed not only through the taverns but also through the center of another German tradition, the beer garden, or more appropriately called by Germans, "the biergarten," and through private clubs and singing societies like the Maennerchor, the Liederkrantz, the Germania, the Workingman's Singing Society, the Columbus Damenchor, the Edelweiss Damenchor (the Swiss), the Helvetta Maennerchor and the German's Butchers Singing Society.

The Maennerchor (men's chorus) was born on October 24, 1848, by twelve men in the German community. The Maennerchor rented rooms,

The Rathskeller in the Maennerchor was a popular gathering spot for more than eighty years. *PC.*

halls, private homes and even attics to practice singing every Tuesday night. For ten years, they met at the Germania Hall on the southeast corner of Main and Fourth in a building erected for them by the Zettlers. Members met to continue a singing tradition that was a hallmark of German-speaking populations. In 1921, they purchased the rectory of the German Independent Protestant Church, an 1880s house owned by the Reverend John Meyer, on South High Street. The church was located at 72 East Mound, near the Jury Room.

Germany did not exist as a country in the 1840s, and in fact, much of Europe was in the midst of revolution in the aftermath of Napoleon. Germans who came to America left an imaginary or virtual homeland that existed only in the mind. In reality, what was to become Germany was made up of provinces, independent cities, principalities and other small political nodes scattered throughout Central Europe. Over 250 small political divisions, most of which had not changed in shape, inheritance laws or official religion since the Reformation had only one commonality—a language. German-speaking areas stretched from the present-day Russia, as far north as St. Petersburg, to southern Poland—not including the German-speaking Austrians of the large Austro-Hungarian Empire.

Having no country or participatory political life of any kind, Germans were bound together by literature, poetry, leider (song) and a fondness for military music. They also were caught up in the revolutionary movement of romanticism that had followed the age of rationalism. Rationalism and the scientific revolution are closely allied. Rationalism influenced America's founding fathers. The Declaration of Independence is a document of "scientific" and rational principles that spells out how facts (coming from the Creator)—not ideals—work. Natural laws and inalienable rights were byproducts of rationalism.

Romanticism, however, was very different. This was the to-be-expected philosophical backlash to rationalism. Romanticism was a movement in which the forces of nature were held in awe, the ideas of a mythological past were glorified and not everything could be rationalized. Some things could only be intuitively felt, and passionate connections with a daffodil (the poet, Wordsworth), death (the Cemetery Beautiful Movement that inspired Green Lawn Cemetery) or one's country (the poet, Longfellow) could be liberating, inspiring or maudlin. Think of Richard Wagner's opera the *Ring of the Nibelungen*, where Rhine maidens cavort, the gods argue over gold versus family ties in their CEO headquarters of Valhalla and the Valkyries ride to the soaring music sometimes hummed by people who think it is from Bugs Bunny's "Kill the Wabbit" cartoon.

The romantic movement included a newly fabricated and, what would prove to be, deadly "ism." Not the same as patriotism, nationalism was the belief that a nation could be defined by a people who were of "the same blood." In contrast to the founding ideals of America that made citizenship a voluntary act for new immigrants (citizenship of land, not blood rights). Intense nationalism led to World War I, and blind nationalism was used to explain allegiance to totalitarianism prior to World War II.

Nationalism in the nineteenth century would eventually create Italy and Germany, and it also was a rallying point for politics in the arts—especially in the literary, musical and visual arts. Nationalism gave rise to folk dance companies and a keen attention to folk costumes, which were a way of pronouncing differences among the 250 German-speaking areas, as well as creating distinctions among villages and regions in central and eastern

Der Munich Restaurant was located in the Rankin Building at 22 West Gay Street, as seen in this 1909 photo, and it was later relocated to be part of the Kaiserhof Hotel at 22 West Mound. *CML.*

Europe. Contrary to common belief, folk costumes do not date to medieval times, unless there had been such a fashion trend as folk rags.

In Columbus, the statue of the famous German poet Frederick Schiller in Schiller Park is a perfect example of two great forces coming together—the romantic notion of an ideal nation which had not yet happened (in Germany) and the promise of a new patriotism for a real country that could be embraced (the United States). That the statue was made in Europe and dedicated during a Fourth of July celebration is no accident. It was not incidental that the park was named for a poet—because language in all its forms, such as poetry and singing—were what united Germans regardless of origin. Schiller Park had formerly been private land, Steward's Grove, used by the Germans for picnics, sporting events and, especially, target shooting contests.

Wherever Germans gathered and drank, all three "isms," products of historical change, were present—romanticism, rationalism and nationalism. It was the nineteenth-century version of a present-day sports bar. Since the advent of CSPN Sports and 24/7 sports coverage, The Ohio State University has become the "Buckeye Nation," fueled by the romantic notion that fans can bond to share scarlet (and gray) blood willingly shed for victory and, under attack from opposing forces and eminent defeat, can use rationalism to explain any diversions from the norm of victory. (This also works for the Irish experience with some modifications.)

The main entrance of Schiller Park, as seen in 1908. Schiller's statue, dedicated on a fourth of July, is tied to German's drinking culture. *CML.*

The Capital City's Most Storied Saloons

German singing societies were cultural outgrowths of the German experience, but in the United States, they were welcomed by Germans and other groups (who supported them as audiences) because the act of community bonding was also safely within the growing middle-class values of the mid nineteenth century. (Again, sort of like present-day sports bars.) At one level, the societies were an extension of the language all Germans could share, and at another level, they represented respectable values, like marriage, family and morals, which were highly regarded. It was all about the appearance of order. This included beer drinking as respectable and socially correct.

The German community, especially, felt that one should expect that privies would be in good repair. Real streets had a defined curb to separate the street from the walkway, the private property lines from the public way. No swearing was permitted in public. Mad dogs would not be allowed to run about. And there would be no "immorality after 10:00 p.m." Was some immorality allowed *before* 10:00 p.m.?

In the 1840s, there were opportunities for skilled workers to come to Columbus. Some manufacturing jobs were available, and people acted as their own small company (shoemakers, broom makers and blacksmiths) in addition to seeking industrial employment.

Sue Gall, a resident of German Village, owner of the Hey-Hey Bar and Grill and formerly with the Maennerchor, said her husband's grandfather was recruited from Germany as a teenager to work in the Columbus breweries.

Nineteenth-century occupations often required workers to have several skill sets to see them through hard times. It is estimated that one out of every five Americans born before the Civil War went bankrupt at some time in their life and had to reinvent themselves to go on.

Who fit the skill set better for both respectability and employability than the Germans? Whether they were Protestant, Jewish or Catholic, Germans were seen as hardworking. The Irish were hard working, but mirthful and far too Catholic to meet both criteria—their trial period for being judged by others was much longer. Of course, this was aided by the fact the Germans and their descendants were beginning to outnumber every other ethnic group in Columbus.

The Germans were also becoming more noticeable. The city directories of the mid-nineteenth century show that of the people listed in Columbus, two Germans emerge as powerhouses—Conrad Born and Louis Hoster. Both were associated with breweries and politics.

OF ALL THE GOOD ONES
THESE ARE BEST

HOSTER'S WIENER
BORN'S XX PALE
SCHLEE'S ELK BREW
COLUMBUS SELECT

An early ad for Hoster Beer. The Hoster and Born families, early brewers, influenced Columbus politics. *CML.*

In 1846, five wards were created in Columbus to administer city government, and "Little Germany," part of which remains today as German Village, was the Fifth Ward. At the same time, there were, in one year in the 1840s, eleven thousand new people arriving in the city, though many would move further west. In 1843, there were three German public schools, two voluntary military companies and several German language newspapers.

The Capital City's Most Storied Saloons

With the new German arrivals, increased because of the revolutions across Europe in 1848, singing societies swelled in membership as popular cultural outlets, but they also functioned as benevolent societies. Membership helped to pay the costs for those in need. They also functioned as social, business and political networks—and all of this co-mingled with German beers and the traditions of the drinking establishments.

The Germans gave Columbus a university: Capital University, which started on North High as a theological seminary. They also contributed beer, grade schools and a kindergarten, beer gardens, shotgun houses, numerous breweries, a cafeteria of religious choices (Catholic, Lutheran, Independent Protestant and Jewish) and a need to figure out refrigeration for the creation of lager beers. Later in the nineteenth century, another brewer, August Wagner, would oversee an eight-million-dollar industry and contribute generously to all of the city's religious charitable organizations.

Where Columbus brewers' money helped the city, Worthington lost a college over a glass of alcohol. The Reverend Philander Chase, uncle of Governor Salmon Chase, was a total abstainer and refused to tolerate drinking among his associates. Chase, annoyed by Worthington founder James Kilbourne's alcoholic breath, secured funds to move the Worthington College to Gambier, Ohio, where it became Kenyon College.

Regarding beer and shotgun houses, and feeling the need to comment on architecture, let the record stand here that these small houses (where interior rooms and their doorways aligned from the front door to the back door) were not named because someone could stand at the front door and fire a shotgun through to the backdoor. Why would anyone do that? Why not shoot a rubber band or hurl a dagger? Just how much liquor did people think was consumed in those days?

Shotgun houses are a style that evolved from Haiti and became popular in New Orleans, and whether they are made of simple stucco and straw or wood or brick, a shotgun is an economical workingman's cottage with few unnecessary passages like halls. The style flourished in early New Orleans among a large population of freed blacks. They built their houses in the style remembered from their grandparents and great grandparents—a style which traveled up the Mississippi River (think of how jazz moved as an art form) and the Ohio and the Scioto Rivers, until it reached Columbus, one of the northern-most places it flourishes. "Shotgun" was never the original term, but it was what many thought was being said; the original word sounded more like "sho gun" (long o sound) and is a West African word for "house."

Yes, German Village is populated by small West African houses on the outskirts of breweries, and Italian Village could have been named Irish Village because the Irish lived near the railroads, the buggy factories, the foundries and the mud holes of Harbor Road (Cleveland Avenue) just outside of the city limits.

The Irish had been part of Columbus history from the very beginning of its roots in the 1797 settlement of Franklinton. Lucas Sullivant was from a family in County Cork, Ireland, whose name was originally Sullivan.

German life was centered on the South Side of Columbus, and the many Irish lived close to Flytown, the low-income area north, and the Badlands, the low-income area stretching from Long Street all the way to Harbor Road. Naghten Street was the so-called Irish Broadway.

The largest migration of Irish immigrants arrived in Boston and New York in the 1840s, escaping the potato blight and the Great Famine in Ireland. They landed in old and filthy clothes, emaciated and near death, on coffin ships. At first, upper class Bostonians laughed at their appearance, but they soon had to take serious notice. One million arrived, and it was the first time America experienced a wave of poor people. A social revolution was brewing.

The Irish would work for anything. The new arrivals congregated in makeshift slums, moving from Boston into New York, and eventually, many

The sons of Franklinton settler Lucas Sullivant helped fuel Columbus's cultural and business growth. Left to right: Joseph (1809–1882), Michael Lucas (1807–1879) and William Starling Sullivant (1803–1873). *CML*.

moved on to Ohio (by way of Cincinnati) and on to Columbus. They followed the building of the canals into Columbus, congregating in tight neighborhoods bound by custom and religion.

They did not bring the Catholic faith to Ohio (actually the first Catholics were the Delaware and Wyandot tribes who had been baptized by the French Jesuits), but they came in such numbers that Catholicism suddenly threatened to become the predominant religion in America. Catholics were already in Kentucky in the late eighteenth century, and a new diocese was established in Bardstown, Kentucky.

When the new bishop of Bardstown, Bishop Flaget, visited Columbus in 1815, he found about fifty Catholic families, many of them Irish. He was convinced that without priests in the area, these "strayed sheep" were destined to become part of the Methodist or Baptists flocks. (That the Catholic faith had an interesting history on the frontier is without question. In the 1820s, Michigan had twelve thousand Catholics made up of Europeans, Native Americans and French and only one priest—he also had six thousand Catholics in Cincinnati and four churches in Ohio, which included a warehouse in Zanesville called Holy Trinity.)

When the next bishop, Bishop Fenwick, succumbed to cholera in a hotel room in Wooster, Ohio, while journeying to small Catholic congregations, his successor had more challenges than ministering to strayed sheep. Bishop John Baptist Purcell was an out-and-out Irishman from County Cork, Ireland—a traveler and a university professor.

Irish laborers had come into the interior of the state to build the canals, the National Road and the railroads about the same time that Bishop Purcell, in an effort to strengthen the chance for a future Diocese of Columbus, brought teaching orders from Belgium to Ohio in the 1840s. Travelling Dominican priests served Mass in Columbus taverns. For Purcell, the timing of his efforts at the same time the Irish laborers arrived was both good news and bad news.

The good news was that an influx of Catholic Irish would make the likelihood of a future Diocese in Columbus more likely. The bad news was this was happening in areas that had previously been predominately Protestant.

The Irish were marked by their brogue and their willingness to undercut prevailing wages. Having arrived with the misfortunes of the Potato Famine, they and their churches became victims of arson and rioting. Irish churches in Perry County were burned, postmasters in Ohio took it upon themselves to destroy Catholic newspapers, a mob attacked a convent in Chillicothe and the future bishop of Columbus, Sylvester Rosecrans

Bishop Sylvester Horton Rosecrans was appointed the first bishop of the newly formed Columbus Catholic Diocese in 1868 and was a major force in defending Irish and German rights. *CML.*

(buried in St. Joseph's undercroft), saved the delegate of Pope Pius IX from a mob in Cincinnati. Near Columbus, in the little town of Somerset, a man was killed by a mob, inflamed by drink, who cried out to kill the damned Irish.

Germans influenced most of the Catholic churches in Columbus. Holy Cross was the new name chosen for Columbus's first Catholic church, St. Remigius, on the same site in the 1840s. But Mass was said in German, and the Irish longed for an English-speaking church of their own. St. Patrick Parish, the second parish in Columbus, was established in 1852 for the English-speaking, predominately Irish, Catholics. (St. Mary's Parish in German Village was established in 1865.)

Other Irish settlements were relatively close by St. Patrick's—Flytown; the Badlands; Milo Grogan, once called the Goose Pond; the Frog Heaven at Grant and State; and Tin Town, a slum next to the Scioto River, near the walls of the Ohio Penitentiary.

Because Catholics tended to be either Germans or Irish (and sometimes not always in agreement with each other), when the time came to build St. Joseph's Cathedral, it should be noted that, first, it was on prime real estate on East Broad Street—to put Columbus on notice that, indeed, the Catholics had arrived to take their place with main line Protestant churches. Secondly, the site was almost equal distance between St. Patrick's and St.

Mary's—like an unofficial "demilitarized zone," where differences in cultural interpretations of the faith between the Irish and the Germans could coexist.

Non-Catholic Columbus citizens grumbled about the cost of a cathedral made of chiseled Licking County sandstone and Pickaway County limestone. Why did the Irish and Germans, who were the workmen in the sewers, ditches and gas works; the errand boys; the seamstresses; and the servant girls need such a costly church? Some Columbus citizens seemed to think the Germans were as poor as the Irish. The bishop replied that Jesus had forgotten about himself in his sacrifices for others—the church was the home for the Holy Sacrament that Jesus did not have time to build—and the Catholics would build it for him.

When the cathedral was completed enough for consecration in 1878, Archbishop Purcell was asked to address the faithful. In a voice weakened by age and emotion, the Archbishop recalled how over forty years before, he had offered Mass in a saloon near the canal.

Germans and Irish did not always exist in peaceful rivalries, but both used the cathedral, and both were well respected in government, supporters of the Democratic Party and counted upon to do the right thing for working families.

Two of the many politically active Irish were Billy Naghten and Patrick Egan. Naghten was the first Irish-Catholic president of Columbus City Council. He was popular and served in 1868–69. In 1870, he was tragically killed when he was hit by a streetcar near the establishment that would become the Flat Iron. North Public Lane was renamed Naghten Street in his honor.

Patrick Egan was a politician and coroner (and a founder of the Egan Ryan funeral homes). In the nineteenth century, the Columbus Irish "invented" St. Patrick's Day because of Egan, and they made the once-solely religious holiday popular among non-Irish.

Egan's livery and business was at 22 West Naghten, very near the present Char-Bar. It was somewhat of a tradition for the Irish of Columbus to meet on March 17 on the lawn of the statehouse after Mass. Here they exchanged information about families from the old country—whose sister married whom, what was happening back in County Cork, who was born and who had died. One March 17, Egan came by with his wagon pulled by a white horse, and the crowd spontaneously called out to him and then began to follow him down the street. A parade was born.

By the next year, when Egan's wagon and horse showed up again, he was followed by the Irish Benevolent Society, the priests of St. Patrick's Church,

Founded in 1859, P.A. Egan Undertaking and Livery is seen in this 1912 photo. The Egans and St. Patrick's Day are linked. Egan's beautiful wagon and horse accidentally started the first St. Patrick's Day parade when it passed by the Statehouse on March 17, where Irish residents gathered to exchange news from letters from Ireland. *CML.*

Bishop Rosecrans himself, the Montgomery Guards (a predominately Irish voluntary military unit who fought in the Mexican War) and the St. Joseph Benevolent Society, who carried banners with their mission statement—"We visit our sick and bury our dead." The Irish Temperance Society also marched—both members. (The Flat Iron has historically been the epicenter of recent St. Patrick's Day activities, and in the past, the parade has marched right in through one door and out the other.)

When other residents abandoned the city during the cholera outbreaks of the 1840s and 1870s, the Irish distinguished themselves because they stayed behind to help others as both individuals and as part of religious orders. Teaching and nursing orders, such as the Sisters of the Poor of St. Francis and the Dominican Sisters of St. Mary's of the Spring, came to Columbus, even in the face of nativist opposition.

The Flat Iron was once Higgins Grocery and Saloon, built in 1914. Higgins took its name from its builder, Herbert Aloysius Higgins, a grocery store clerk who made good. He was, however, always known as Myrt, short for Myrtle, a nickname from childhood when he had long blonde curls and looked like a girl. Before the building of the popular flat iron-shaped building, there had been several other buildings on the site. Higgins built a flatiron building that was just eight feet wide on one end and twenty-five feet on the other. It was a way to maximize an oddly shaped parcel of land. He proved to be a popular grocery and saloon owner (and owner of the last remaining saloon of Irish Broadway). He extended credit to his regulars, kept the bar open whenever he could to accommodate the unusual schedules of the circus workers and the railroad men and was mourned on the first St. Patrick's Day after his death. The parade marchers took off their hats and observed a moment of silence as they passed Higgins Grocery and Saloon.

Flatiron buildings are iconic. The most famous flatiron building is in New York, and its popularity was created by artists and early photographers who were fascinated by its look, especially in rainy and foggy weather. It opened in October 1902 and was originally called the Fuller Building, for the Fuller Real Estate Company. Its unusual shape was created because Fifth Avenue and Broadway intersected at an angle, leaving a piece of land shaped like an

The unique shape of the Higgins Building (now Flatiron) is seen in this 1990 photo. *CML.*

iron. The New York Flatiron demolished several old buildings to create one skyscraper with more than twenty floors to fill the site, designed by famed Chicago architect, Daniel Burnham.

Though it was not the first skyscraper in New York, it was the first uptown skyscraper and very controversial. The first concern was no one was sure that steel was really a tested material and would be stronger than iron. The second concern was both safety and moral. The height of the building at this corner created wind shears that knocked people off their feet and made women's skirts fly over their heads. No doubt it became the dandies' favorite corner for this very reason. Columbus's building is far smaller, with no wind shears, but it does have a mystery. It was originally described as four stories, but appears to be only three. Despite an unusually deep basement, there is no indication it was ever a street-level story that became entombed by a raised street bed.

Burnham did not design the Flatiron in Columbus, but he did design the Wyandotte Building, Columbus's first skyscraper, and the Union Station, whose demise in the 1970s created the Columbus Landmarks Foundation. Many railroads converged just outside the establishment on the other side of Naghten: the Columbus and Xenia Railroad, the Pennsylvania Railroad, the Baltimore and Ohio Railroad and the New York Railroad. One set of the train tracks actually ran within a few feet of Higgins Grocery and Saloon. Fortunately, at the time, the grocery portion of the building was where the bar is today, and the bar was where the restaurant is today. This meant that departing patrons who had a little too much to drink had a chance to avoid the train. A stairway that led downstairs was in the middle of the establishment, and rooms to let were upstairs.

In addition to needing warehouses for storage of goods arriving or leaving the depot, railroads were dependent on hotels for passengers who needed a room or a drink. There were many small hotels down the street—the Manhattan, the Waldo, the Ohio and the Arcade—some respectable and clean, others not so much.

Those who remember the original location of the Daniel Burnham-designed Union Station on High Street might not remember that this was only the elaborate façade of the station, and the trains arrived and departed some distance to the east. Those who know only the remnant of the sole-remaining arch may not even realize the arch was moved twice before arriving at its present home at Burnham Park (get it?) in the Arena District.

East of High Street and across from Higgins Grocery and Saloon were the freight yards, which moved produce, goods and even circus animals. Irish men did whatever extra work they could, working as haulers and animal wranglers. There are only a few warehouses left on Fifth and Neilston Streets that remain; most have come down for Ross Labs or Columbus State University, and along with them, the original taverns disappeared. It was a workingman's neighborhood, and it was said that one could get a paycheck from the railroads or the buggy works on a Friday night and drink it away slowly at each saloon until one arrived at St. Patrick's Church on Sunday morning. The John Deere Plow company and the Dean and Berry paint company were other Higgins neighbors.

Though the Irish neighborhood shared a border with the Badlands, a racially mixed neighborhood, the commonality of the two neighborhoods was poverty. Visitors to Columbus, if they visited the warehouses south of the depot, were often surprised to find so many poor people (well into the twentieth century) living there. The Badlands had a "charm" of its own.

Self-appointed mayor and ward healer of the area "Smokey" Alexander Hobbs ran numbers games, saloons, dives and an opium den that attracted a number of curious and rich young men from the East Side. By the early 1870s, the population of Columbus rose to over 31,000 people, and the African American population, who had always been part of the original settlements, doubled to almost 1,800. Five political wards in the city grew to nine wards. Many blacks lived in the First Ward, near Long and Gay Streets around High (the start of the Badlands), though blacks were spread across the city (and outside the city limits) in a variety of communities.

Drinking customs were dictated by ethnic origin and socioeconomics. In the Badlands, drinking was associated with gambling, drugs and prostitution. In the first years of the twentieth century, police reported that they had arrested two hundred girls under the age of fourteen for prostitution on the eastern edge of the Badlands near Fort Hayes. Whereas fifty years before, Harbor Road (Cleveland Avenue) had been a known route on the Underground Railroad, now the street near the military barracks was filled with cheap saloons and dives. The Irish had their men's drinking establishments, where drinking was done at the bar, and there were no stools. However, Germans also enjoyed the beer gardens, which were family-oriented, with tables, chairs, linens (even napkins) and food. The Irish tended to regard the saloon as a men's establishment where they could hunch over a bit of lunch and a beer with no time to sit and relax at a table.

Hotels began to appear in Columbus in the middle of the nineteenth century, and they varied a great deal in size and services. They could

The historic Great Southern Fireproof Hotel was opened in 1897 and hosted important guests from President Roosevelt to President Obama. *CML.*

be respectable and revered old hostelries used primarily by families or travelers, have bars and dining rooms that appealed to members of the Ohio legislature or cater to a certain clientele—farmers coming in for market days or temperance hotels for reformers and abolitionists. Others advertised with interesting names. The Stag Turkish Bath and Hotel was clearly a men's hotel and bar with a reputation for frequent liquor violations and illegal gambling.

At the turn of the twentieth century, Columbus had thirty-two downtown hotels, and some would be known even into the twentieth century, such as the Neil House, the Deshler, the Chittenden, the Hartman and the Normandie. The Capital, the Buckeye House and the American House Hotel were well established before the Civil War. Others, like Smith's European Hotel on the corner of Broad and High, lasted into very recent times, though they had been covered over by multiple façades that obscured the original building.

Of all the hotels mentioned, only one of them, the Great Southern or the Westin Great Southern Hotel, remains downtown and holds a special place in the history of taverns in Columbus. Designed by the well-known architectural firm of Yost and Packard, it opened on August 23, 1897, and would include the Southern Theater, Columbus's oldest remaining nineteenth-century theater. The Southern was the first fireproof hotel, an important new development when fires often destroyed theaters and hotels.

The Southern is important for three reasons: It made a statement about the prosperity and importance of the German community, who saw themselves as now being part of the movers and shakers; it had a rooftop beer garden that brought a traditional German drinking custom into the mainstream; and it had a gimmick—the oyster bar.

Inside the lobby of the Westin Great Southern, next to the Thurber Bar (Columbus favorite son and humorist James Thurber's mother and brother lived in the hotel in the 1940s and 1950s), is a founders' plaque. All the names are German—a who's who of the community—and a closer look indicates that among the partnership are German Catholics, German Jews and German Protestants, and there is only one other name, an Irishman who was the contractor.

The rooftop garden was a popular fad in New York at the turn of the twentieth century—it made sense in stifling summers and seemed both bohemian and elegant. New York's Waldorf-Astoria spent fifty thousand

The Great Southern Hotel roof garden opened two years after the hotel, as seen in 1899. *CML.*

dollars a year on flowers for their rooftop garden, and patrons sat among ivy-covered pergolas and cascades of honeysuckle. The Southern Hotel's rooftop garden was decorated with electric lights strung from poles, the requisite greenery and the occasional presence of President William McKinley and members of his cabinet.

While a McKinley sighting was not quite the same as catching a peek at New York's scandalous and beautiful Evelyn Nesbit dining on a rooftop garden, McKinley was, nevertheless, on the A list of celebrity sightings when he was in Columbus. On the other hand, McKinley might have been overshadowed by Evelyn's presence had the two ever met.

Evelyn Nesbitt had the rock star status of her day, and Columbus newspapers eagerly followed the scandalous events of her life. Her millionaire husband, Henry Thaw, had followed architect Stanford White to the rooftop garden of the Madison Square Garden Theater, which White had designed (as the papers liked to point out) on a warm June evening in 1907 to pump three bullets into him for having an illicit affair with Evelyn. The juicy details included Evelyn's signature come-on, swinging on a red velvet swing in the boudoir in her undies, something McKinley would never have done.

The Great Southern Hotel's rooftop garden was a combination of elegance and German tradition (this was, after all, a very German establishment) and made drinking very respectable. The view of Columbus from the top of the Southern also made it a very popular place, until the smokestacks of the hotel caused the guests' clothes to smell and their eyes to water. The rooftop garden lasted only a few years.

An oyster bar was the foodie gimmick of the day and is worth mentioning, not because the word "bar" appears in the name, but because what started as a simple fare in the East to accompany drinks grew into an obsession that accompanied drinking. If rooftop gardens were literally and metaphorically on the top of a hotel's draw, oyster bars once started in the basement in the nineteenth century—the oyster cellar.

An oyster house, oyster bar or oyster cellar was the source of nibble bar food. Oyster madness took over America in the 1880s. Annual consumption of oysters in America was 660 oysters per person—and how many Americans never saw or ate an oyster? The oyster house or oyster bar became a specialized restaurant in Chicago, New York, Boston, Denver, St. Louis, Louisville and Cincinnati—wait, Cincinnati? St. Louis? Denver? How far from the ocean were these places? And if Cincinnati had one—well then, Columbus had to have one too.

Grand Central Oyster Bar, in New York City, was the epitome of what Smith's European Hotel and the Great Southern Hotel wanted to be. *PC.*

The oyster bar was a gimmick—the standing fully-cooked bear of its day—and it was an excuse to indulge in seafood, game and, especially, the choicest ales, wines and brandies. The size of the oyster was a draw. A plate of ten- or eleven-inch-long oysters gave bragging rights to the consumer. But the fact that the bivalves were even on a plate in Columbus, Ohio, was also a draw—their presence implied extravagance and technological advances of the Gilded Age, the post–Civil War's gift to the North that proved divine providence had meant for them to win the war.

Oysters would be shelled, packed in milk containers and shipped to Columbus, where they would be placed back in the half shell—the freshness was dependent on the timely arrivals and departures of the railroad, and year-round availability of ice was becoming less a novelty because of improvements in refrigeration. Imported fresh (or hopefully fresh) oysters from the Eastern seaboard were delivered to Smith's European Hotel on the corner of Broad and High, and the Great Southern Hotel, the two most popular oyster bars in Columbus.

Not to be outdone, the American Saloon (under the American Hotel) advertised fresh oysters kept constantly on hand for all seasons, and, in addition, offered birds, venison, fresh fish, sardines, pickled oysters, clams and lobsters and the purest liquors, wines, cordials and "segars." Oysters could be obtained by the dozen, hundred or by the can. The State House and Saloon and Restaurant (located between the American House and the Neil House) offered everything the American Saloon offered, but it also included poached eggs, rarebits, steaks, tea, coffee and chocolate all hours of the day and evening. It, too, offered confectionary and "segars," along with foreign, eastern and city papers in the saloon. The City Saloon, at the corner of High Street and Surgar Alley, offered the same exotic food, but perhaps knowing that oysters were also considered an aphrodisiac, it also advertised that it had "added several private rooms for gentlemen wishing to give suppers." On draught were Carew's Detroit Ale, Schultz XX Pale Ale and Scotch Ale. More modestly, the Neil House Saloon offered "fresh oysters and all the luxuries of the season, served daily, at the Neil House Saloon, by Harry."

Though the Germans and other Central European groups had drinking customs that frequently centered on meals shared with the entire family, the Irish drank differently. While Germans drank in the company of family, Irish men drank at the bar in the companionship of their gender. Irish women and children did not frequent saloons; when they were in saloons, the women and children were helping to run them.

This is well documented by the history of the Main Bar at 16 West Main Street. Though building records are vague about the exact age of this nineteenth-century building, it is survivor set in a neighborhood of atmosphere—including the Irish and German experiences, the canal warehouse district, a hanging gallows, a Chinatown and purloined medical specimens. The building's interior remains relatively intact, but the basement has been swallowed by repeated sewer and infrastructure improvements.

Prior to Prohibition, Columbus had almost 500 saloons downtown: 469 licensed ones, to be exact. Twenty-three were in a three-block radius around the Main Bar. Like many of its neighbors, the Main Bar was listed as both a dwelling and a saloon or a boardinghouse and saloon.

Mrs. Francis Jones ran the establishment in 1911, Mrs. Carrie Martin ran the boardinghouse and saloon (selling soft drinks in Prohibition) from the 1920s through 1930s and Mrs. Duey ran the saloon in 1933. Husbands worked at laboring jobs as haulers or draymen while their wives tended bar. Daughters acted as maids and servers. The tavern keepers and the

The Main Bar today at 16 West Main Street, a survivor of nineteenth-century taverns in Columbus. *SB.*

boardinghouse operators did not appear to be the owners of the buildings, but rather they were only the tenants, and to pay the rent, everyone was expected to participate.

In the nineteenth century, near the Main Bar were Gottlob Waidger's saloon and the Little Southern Café. Down the street and toward the river was the city's first prison—little more than a small building with most of the cells in the basement. They were muddy and infested with the river's ubiquitous rat population. Once, the gallows stood near the canal (now Waterford Tower). Death was no stranger here, as the Indian mounds were also nearby. The Main Bar stands a short distance from the original gallows site, and part of the Main Bar's appeal is the neighborhood's history.

Efforts to stop capital punishment in Ohio were introduced as far back as the 1840s, and other states had already banned hangings. The Ohio effort to reform was not sincere, however; it was a political football of the Ohio Legislature. Capital punishment was carried out in public. On February 9, 1844, there was a sensational event planned for Columbus residents: a double hanging, and one of the victims was a woman. William Graham, a white convicted criminal, and Hester Foster, a young African American woman who allegedly tried to kill a white female convict while in prison, were to be hanged. There was no record of a trial for Foster or even a trial for whatever crime she committed that put her into the jail.

On the day of the hanging, a Franklinton blacksmith, Sullivan Sweet, was part of the crowd of an estimated two thousand people who gathered to watch this event that was equal parts public justice, curiosity and entertainment. Sweet was trampled to death by a horse after the crowd pushed and shoved for viewing spots. The crowd was so unruly and the fear of mob violence was so great that it prompted the citizens of Columbus to introduce a bill to ban public hangings. The bill was not to abolish hangings—just hangings in public.

Executions moved inside the Ohio Penitentiary on Spring Street, but not before one more grisly twist to the story. Graham's body was dug up by local doctor Icabod Jones and his assistant. The body was most likely destined for dissection, because Jones proudly kept Graham's foot preserved in alcohol

Club 185 is long associated with residents of the German neighborhood, and regulars are seen here in mourning for a regular who was murdered outside the bar. *CD.*

for many years at his Town Street office. No one is sure where Hester Foster's body was buried, probably in an unmarked grave near the gallows.

Unlike historic taverns in other parts of the city, the Main Bar is a rare snapshot of both late nineteenth-century and early twentieth-century Columbus. Often, present-day upscale taverns have kept their past lives a secret.

Annie Kaisers was a neighborhood saloon. Only a generation or two ago, small children were sent there to bring home beer in a bucket called a "growler." No one asked for a note. Husbands sneaked around the block to enter the back door, unseen by their wives. Not far away, the Rose Garden was once known in the neighborhood as "the bucket of blood," for the many altercations that spilled into the street. In the neighborhood of Annie Kaisers and the Rose Garden, in the 1950s, fifty-four bars and saloons operated next to homes, barber shops, beauty salons, saw companies, auto repairs and candy shops. In the bar, men drank a beer and watched wrestling or

Club185 as seen today at 185 East Livingston Avenue—no longer just a neighborhood bar and certainly not the plumbing store and family residence it once was. *PC.*

soap operas. No accordion music was piped in. The difference among the three—the Main Bar, Annie Kaisers and the Rose Garden—is time and location. Annie Kaisers became Max and Erma's on South Third Street, and the Rose Garden evolved into Lindy's on South Fifth Street, both in German Village.

Club 185 also has had a makeover. A neighborhood bar for over thirty years, Club 185 had a jukebox in the corner and patrons who looked out for each other. Few patrons of today's Club 185 know the sad story of a regular who walked out of the bar on a rainy evening and was mysteriously murdered. There is no memory of this unsolved murder of a quiet woman, just outside the front door. A regular patron, her life is as little remembered as the history of the building—a cigar store, a hairdresser, an apartment house upstairs and a plumber's business in the back, an auction house, a café, a used furniture store, furnished rooms to let and a barber shop. Nearby was Margulis Department Store (most recently a video store) and the Progressive Holiness Church. It has had its cycle of families, immigrants, craftsmen, businesses and taverns.

Chapter *3*

Brothers in Arms, Brothers at War

The Exclusive World of Men

Grant served as quartermaster during the Mexican War. He took it into his own hands to get into the fight. He was sympathetic to the Mexicans and impressed by the country's natural beauty. After his presidency he would be involved with the building of a railroad from Mexico City to the Rio Grande, but it would be another of his business failures. Grant and Julia were married soon after the Mexican War ended in 1848, James Longstreet, a West Point and Mexico comrade before he became a Confederate general, was a groomsman. The match was very much a love match, and Julia threw herself into making military life less dreary for Grant, In light of his later, notorious reputation for hitting the bottle, it is startling that he was president of the Sons of Temperance lodge while posted to Sackets Harbor, New York.
—David Hardin. After the War. *Ivan R. Dee: Lanham, Maryland. 2010*

Bohemian
Hop-flavored
Puritan Malt
Richest, Strongest, Best
High in Quality
Ask Any Dealer
—Columbus Citizen *advertisement, March 12, 1924*

Newspapers Hold Referendum on Prohibition. Prohibition has been the law of the land for seven years. Yet the debate rages in Washington and

in millions of homes on the question, "Can it be enforced or should it be modified? The Newspaper Enterprise Association, the biggest newspaper feature service in the country, has asked The Citizen to co-operate with more than 700 daily newspaper coast to coast to see what people think.
—Columbus Citizen, *March 9, 1926*

From President Ulysses S. Grant's term of office to President Warren G. Harding's term of office is time long enough to observe changing values. Grant himself struggled with drink. Entrepreneurs looked for new ways to market something to satisfy public demands for alcohol in the wake of temperance movements, and straw polls showed that the American public had many diverging ideas about alcohol consumption.

More than eighty years is also the length of time represented by three historic tavern styles that represent three distinctive periods in liquor consumption: the frontier tavern and boardinghouse, the opulent Victorian bar and billiards palace and the Arts and Crafts style smoke-filled bohemian nook.

The Jury Room, the Elevator Brewery and the Ringside Tavern all continue to exist, but their origins span a hundred years of eras and styles related to taste, public opinion and architecture.

They also share more than lucky longevity. They were essentially products of the all-male society that dominated the nineteenth and much of the twentieth century. Their locations, architecture and history of the surrounding neighborhoods help to explain their establishment—and perhaps even their current existence. As extensions of the man's world, each establishment could be associated with the popular sport of the day, including the sport of politics and power, as well as vice. All were affected by the hazards of the city—namely, fires. In some cases, individuals who were associated with one of the three establishments became associated with another of the three, but then, Columbus is like the famous television tavern Cheers, "a place where everybody knows your name."

By its fiftieth birthday, Columbus was emerging as a complex town in a nation of complex politics. A variety of attitudes were emerging over democracy for the common man versus time-honored beliefs that democracy came with the responsibilities of property ownership.

The history of the Jury Room, described in the first chapter, is part tavern and part boardinghouse, reflecting frontier concerns and a young city's struggles with the issues of its day. Its architecture had been utilitarian and evolutionary—a simple brick, Federal-style structure built with a deep foundation for the front, rooms for family or guests upstairs, secondary business

Bott Brothers' exterior entrance, 161 North High, was the epitome of a man's world circa 1900s. *CML.*

for Union and Confederate soldiers in the attached house and, later, an added pressed-tin ceiling to hide burned beams and keep soot out of the beer.

In this tavern, there were topics to discuss—new public cisterns, politics, the novelty of hot air balloon ascensions, politics, the new public bath on Rich Street for men and women (at different times of the day), politics, the shock that a dance academy opened and actually made money teaching waltzes and polkas to men, politics and the recognition that as Columbus was changing, the richer got richer and the poor got slums. Oh, and politics too.

Columbus was born as a political baby, and politics reigned in the man's world of the saloon.

In a town where residents had come from both the South and New England, opinions differed throughout different eras. Though there was a growing movement against slavery in Columbus, encouraged by periodic religious reform and born-again Protestant revival movements, many white people were suspicious of immigrants and free African Americans as citizens. That many in the bar were immigrants was not relevant; they were suspicious of those other immigrants. That the African Americans in Columbus were well-known and accepted community members was not relevant; they were of the community, but not citizens in the eyes of the Ohio legislature.

Don't even ask about women. Despite the fact that women's rights and dress reformer Amelia Bloomer's full-length pantaloons had begun to appear on Columbus streets (the wearers causing quite a stir), everyone knew voting meant one household per vote, not one person. Therefore, critics argued, the convention at Seneca Falls, New York, was misguided. Women had great power and influence at the ballot box because they were the moral authority of the home.

Of course, moral authorities do not need to say much, they just exude principles, and in the nineteenth century, women were often forbidden to speak out publicly. They found their political voice as spiritualists who could communicate with the other world—thanks to the popularity of the Fox sisters in upstate New York, who heard mysterious tapping noises from under their table—and as abolitionists who spoke on the same platform as Frederick Douglass and William Lloyd Garrison.

Temperance suggested that mankind was a creature that could be perfected. Reform movements, especially regarding alcohol consumption, were not, by theological hairsplitting, in the spirit of the Puritans. Puritan ideas were predestination concepts. One was either saved or unsaved, and

Located in Flytown, one of Columbus's colorful slums, First and Last Chance Saloon at 519 West Goodale, as seen in 1916, was owned by Salvatore Presutti. The saloon is typical of the more than three hundred operating at the time. Within the next generation, the Presuttis successfully opened a popular and beloved restaurant in their family home in the Grandview area. It closed in the 1970s. *CML.*

the Creator had long ago set in motion who was who. Reform movements—in all their manifestations—were to be liberating. Free will would set one free from alcohol. Even the Puritans drank. The Pilgrims on the *Mayflower* had carried over ten thousand gallons of beer. Taverns continued to exist despite talk of temperance throughout American history.

The Jury Room remained through new names and new owners. However, the Rose Tavern, the saloon with the Bible verse as part of its sign, had other owners and was known by other names—the Franklin House and later the City House. By the 1850s, some of the very early taverns like the Rose disappeared. It went out with a murder in April 1851. Two friends, George Parcels and Thomas Spencer began the evening with a round of drinks and playful jokes, but for Spencer, the jokes turned into a sort of frenzied horseplay, and he fired a pistol, killing Parcels. Spencer was found guilty of manslaughter, and he was convicted to six years in the penitentiary, though he was later pardoned by the Ohio governor Reuben Woods.

Alcohol and firearms have been a potent combination in every age. Suffice to say, entire volumes could be written about Columbus's saloons and taverns and the violence that followed alcohol-induced passions.

On July 4, 1855, nineteen-year-old Henry Foster was killed near High and Town Streets, the result of tensions over German immigrants and holiday drinking. The German Turnverein (or Turners) traditionally marched as part of the Fourth of July celebrations. Turners were a popular German tradition equivalent to a "sound body, sound mind" movement. Generally, they marched in their own community in South Columbus. This year, they marched downtown to the statehouse. Henry Foster, a young man of Columbus with nativist leanings, and his friends had been throwing stones at passing Germans during the Fourth of July parade. Stone throwing turned to pistols, and Henry Foster was killed, but no one knew who fired the first shot or who killed Foster. No convictions ever occurred, and each side continued to blame the other.

Despite the fact that the Germans were the largest ethnic group in the city (or perhaps because of it), there was backlash in many cities to the growing numbers and the influence of immigrants. Nativist groups felt only the native-born were worthy of American citizenship. In addition to despising immigrants, Catholics, Jews and nativists had no fond feelings for the truly native-born, the American Indian. As equal opportunity haters, it was fitting that their political party was proudly called the Know-Nothings.

In the midst of cholera outbreaks and new immigrants from Ireland and Germany, national events were in the daily conversations of the drinkers outside the numerous taverns and watering holes. The concept of the frontier—an edge between civilization and the uncharted—had rapidly moved westward. The city had moved from being on the edge of the nation's frontier in the 1800–1820s to focusing on issues further west.

Columbus was more a jumping-off point to the West than ever before. In one year, eleven thousand people moved through Columbus—equal to the number of people in the city at that time. Some Columbus residents moved too. A group of Columbus German families moved west where they established New Columbus, Nebraska (now Columbus, Nebraska). William Deshler helped to form Deshler, Nebraska, and the discovery of gold in California in 1848 drew solid citizens and tavern frequenters alike to saddle up and head west.

In the years before the Civil War, Columbus had been described as an "easygoing capital city." Approximately eighteen thousand people lived in Columbus on the eve of the Civil War—far less than the number of students who cross the Oval each day at Ohio State.

There were almost two hundred licensed saloons (which did not include many of the hotels) in the area from North Public Lane (Naghten Street) to South Public Lane (Livingston Avenue) and from the river to Seventh Street (Grant Avenue). The highest concentration was along both sides of South High Street, starting at Town Street and the east side of South Fourth Street—these accounted for almost one-third of the two hundred saloons. In one block along the west side of South High Street, from Rich Street to Friend (Main Street), nine saloons stood next to each other, and others wrapped around the corners.

Columbus was easygoing on the outside, filled with drink and political discourse on the inside and could display a little naughty side, as related in Charles Cole's *A Fragile Capital*. Uriah Heath (yes, the name does sound like a character from a Charles Dickens's novel) was a pious Methodist circuit rider who stayed at the Buckeye House across from the statehouse. Heath recorded in his journal, "Here we saw sin all around us, though the land lord treated us with kindness." The English novelist Charles Dickens found his trip to Columbus and stay at the Neil House rather dull.

Within fifty years of its founding, Columbus was changed by new ideas and new technology more than Columbus changed between the presidencies of Harry Truman and Bill Clinton. In the last half of the twentieth century, cars were still cars, airplanes were still airplanes and telephones were still telephones, but animals were no longer used to eat refuse. Hogs that roamed the city to serve as walking garbage cans were finally impounded by city ordinance in 1862. Hundreds were rounded up within a few days. Columbus had a university, Capital University, and state institutions for the blind, deaf or mentally impaired. The new Green Lawn Cemetery, having opened in 1848, was now being used, and the graves in the old North Graveyard (under the present North Market) were being dismantled.

Vessels still used the feeder canal, but now they might be steam driven. Stagecoaches no longer stopped to pick up passengers at hotels. Both canals and stagecoaches blamed the decline of their businesses on the five railroads that now served Columbus. Twenty-four trains arrived daily. Horse-drawn streetcars began to connect the city, and they would reach from Goodale Park to the taverns and beer gardens near Stewart's Grove (later Schiller Park) by 1864.

The center of Columbus was shifting north toward the depot at Union Station, and hacks, not stages, connected passengers to a new model of hotel with amenities and dining rooms (and napkins!). No surprise, they also served liquor. The American House stood on the northwest corner of State and High Streets (the Vern Rife Center), and farther south was the United States Hotel (the former Lazarus Department Store).

Harp Saloon was located on 85 East Gay Street, with concerts by Joe Arizona, known as the "Great Harp Soloist," circa 1900. "Musical saloon," however, had a different connotation, generally meaning more bawdy music and dancing girls—something to distract patrons so they could be pickpocketed. *CML.*

The second Neil House opened in 1862, after the first hotel burned down in 1860. Its loss was due to low water in the cisterns, and it was a wake-up call that the city needed to focus attention on issues that plagued larger urban centers. With 150 rooms, the second Neil House was amazing—with built-in stores of drugs and clothing, newspaper and barber shops and many places to drink.

But the sectarian nature of pre–Civil War politics was not a good time for the civic action of a new fire department.

The Mexican War in the 1840s showed how transportation and communication advancements were dissolving the parochial natures of rural and urban areas—it was the first American foreign war fought almost entirely on foreign soil (soon to become American soil). It was a war that would determine who had power—the north or the south. The Mexican War was hotly debated in the taverns in Columbus. Almost six thousand Americans were wounded or died in the Mexican War, and twice as many would die of diseases. For the Mexicans, the American victory would destabilize their politics—seven Mexican presidents in two years—and leave a bitter taste for the American invasion.

The issues of the Mexican War were a trial run for the Civil War. What would happen if the balance of power swung in favor of more slave states? Should American interests expand to the Pacific (not a hard decision with many silver and gold deposits in Nevada and California)? Would California be a free state or a slave state? Should Americans be in Texas? This was, after all, not like defending American lives and investments in the War of 1812.

Young men in a tavern on South Third Street discussed these questions over beer. Their sons and veteran graybeards of the Mexican War would discuss the same sectarian issues before the Civil War inside the same tavern. The only thing that had changed was that there was now a newly completed Trinity Lutheran Church across the street.

This era of politics was a world of men—and what better place to discuss politics than in the tavern? Despite Ohio's prominence as a supporter of the Union cause, Columbus tavern goers would have had a variety of opinions on national issues and foreign policy.

Though many residents had New England roots, Southern gentility reigned in parlors and drawing rooms. William Dean Howells, a local boy who would later become editor of *Atlantic Monthly*, commented, on the eve of the Civil War, up and down Columbus were "wide and shady streets… and were called Rich and Town and State and Broad…there were pleasant houses of brick, with or without limestone facings…and showing through their trees the thrilling light of evening parties that burst with the music of dancing from every window."

Many in Columbus had family in slave states. Many Southern-rooted families had come into Ohio with family slaves that were now on salary. They had repudiated the source of the family's wealth. Others in Columbus, like Samuel Medary, a newspaperman and Lincoln hater, was euphemistically called a Peace Democrat. Generally, however, Lincoln's appearance in Columbus en route to Washington was well received.

When the war did come in 1861, all of the quasi-military companies who had taken enormous pride—especially the Germans and the Montgomery Volunteers—organized and drilled to make real war. Goodale Park became Camp Jackson, where 3,500 men lived in hastily constructed barracks or tents. Contracts for ammunition, wagons, rations, religious tracts, bandages and uniforms made many wealthy, except for the prisoners at the Ohio Penitentiary.

Taverns reflected these periods of anxiety, unprecedented growth and dichotomies, but the war did not end in six months as many would have

Union soldiers enjoying a beer and possibly celebrating their mustering out at Camp Jackson, circa 1860s. *CML.*

liked to believe, dragging on from 1861 into 1862, and for three more years, the war made strange bedfellows—and regarding the Jury Room, this was literal, not metaphorical.

During the Civil War, Camp Chase, located four miles west of Columbus on the Hilltop, was intended to be a mustering-in point for forming units into the fifty-five Ohio regiments, a rendezvous for organization and drilling and, later, a mustering-out point for those returning from war.

Near Hague Avenue and West Broad stood the old Four Mile House, a family home that was turned into a tavern. It had been a log cabin, owned by the Bigelows, who had moved from Plain City in 1862 and stayed until after World War I. The log structure was embellished by numerous additions, until the final addition that created one continuous long bar and made it a tavern. During the Civil War, Mrs. Bigelow did more than sell

liquor. She also baked pies to sell to the soldiers for five cents a piece. Pumpkin pies were her specialty. In the 1920s, it was a novelty for visitors to look at the small round hole where a Minié ball was still lodged. It was intended for an escaping Confederate soldier from the nearby Camp Chase, but the Union officer accidentally hit the arm of one of the Bigelow boys who had been sitting on the porch. The bullet passed through his arm and into the porch rail.

Tavern guests in the 1860s would have seen a military camp, established for the training of Union troops, begin to turn into a prisoner of war camp as mounting losses for the South swelled the camp's

Hannah Bigelow and her husband, Timothy, took over as innkeepers of the Four Mile House Inn and Tavern in 1863. *CML.*

Camp Chase, located near Four Mile House at Hague and West Broad, experienced catastrophic deaths due to typhoid in the Civil War. *CML.*

population. Marched out West Broad Street, the arriving prisoners would have been a spectacle. But then again, so was the appearance of Confederate officers on the streets of Columbus.

The war, being a brother's war, after all, meant that Southern gentlemen could be accorded the dignity and presumption that they did not have to be watched every minute.

Confederate officers in uniform began to appear in the shops on High Street, were invited to the legislative sessions at the statehouse (presumably to be re-educated about abolition and states' rights), were seen at the theater and dime museum and frequently participated in the activities in the Neil House, where they favored the city's black barbers. The barbers at the Neil House were particularly skilled in dying graying hair into a more senatorial white.

Little did they realize that many of the free blacks who worked in and around the hotels were newly smuggled arrivals on the Underground Railroad that ran from the Ohio River northward, through downtown and then continued on the old Harbor Road (Cleveland Avenue). They were helped by Columbus's white and black conductors in a secret network that included the janitor at the old City Hall and Thomas Bull, an ardent Clintonville abolitionist. All of the conductors will never be known, but among the most active was John Ward, an African American drayman with his own wagons. (The Ward Furniture and Moving Company is today the oldest continuously owned black business in the United States.) Hidden in plain sight, the presence of runaways in the middle of the war was delicious irony.

At 22 East Mound, the site of the Jury Room, certain nights were given over to the Union officers and the ladies who worked the back of the house, bringing delight and diversion to those in the defense of their country, and on other nights, Confederate officers were permitted to taste the delights of the Columbus ladies. Same ladies, different nights.

War corrupts morality. Liquor excuses it. Saloon keepers defied Sunday closing laws and liquor sales by keeping the back doors open. Alcoholic binging drove some soldiers to vandalism against stores, fruit stands and even violence against Columbus's black citizens.

Alcohol fueled the politics in the middle of the war. Though the Union effort was under the leadership of the Republican Party, the Democratic Party's national convention in Columbus in 1863 underscored deep divisions in the city. Irish and German immigrants in Columbus overwhelmingly supported the more radical of the two Democratic candidates who felt that Lincoln and the Union were heading the country in the wrong direction. They were also concerned about economic competition from freed slaves.

When a Lancaster, Ohio journalist was released from imprisonment for allegedly making seditious statements, he was given a hero's welcome at the Goodale House. Later, prominent Columbus citizens Judge Thurman, Samuel Medary and others made inflammatory toasts in the American Hotel—"Executive proclamations…overthrow the Constitution and the law" and "the Constitution as it is, the Union as it was and the Negroes where they are." Within the month, a group of one hundred Union soldiers from Camp Chase attempted to burn down Medary's newspaper office.

The women at 22 East Mound were either entrepreneurs or fallen daughters. In a nearby township, the adopted daughter of a prominent farmer committed suicide in a bordello north of the city, having been driven out of her home by her relationship with a young Columbus man in uniform.

Camp followers—sometimes women looking to barter sex for money, sometimes young women naively following a sweetheart's promises or still others with babies—became enough of a problem on the road to Camp Chase that eventually, Lucas Sullivant's own house on West Broad was given over for their care. In 1865, the Sisters of the Good Shepherd came to Columbus to take on the care of young women who had gone astray (whether they wanted help or not). Rosemont Center near Sunbury Road is a descendant of this effort.

When the initial twenty-three Confederate prisoners arrived in 1861, no one could have predicted that Camp Chase would be a permanent military prison, holding over nine thousand prisoners in 1865. The initial good care of prisoners in 1861 gave way to lack of prisoner care and outbreaks of typhoid fever. Public bitterness over the war, backlash against Confederates who arrived in prison with their slaves and alarm over attempted Confederate escapes from camp all led to neglect of rations, restrictions and increasingly poor sanitation.

Without adequate protection from the bacteria breeding grounds of raw sewage, diseases could be rampant. Over two thousand Confederate soldiers were buried at Camp Chase, mostly from disease, and when room ran out, they were buried at Green Lawn Cemetery and the East Precinct Graveyard on East Livingston where seventy-five Confederate graves still remain, lost and unmarked.

At the beginning of the war, the town's citizens lived between East Public Lane (Livingston Avenue) and North Public Lane (Naghten Street), eastward along Mount Vernon Avenue and around Washington Avenue. Franklinton was still a separate community. A few people lived beyond the city limits, like William Hubbard, a banker, who lived on High Street near Goodale Street.

By the end of the war, the new northern boundary of the city's population was about East Fifth Avenue and stretching toward the independent town of North Columbus, the site of another Civil War camp, Camp Thomas, near Arcadia Avenue and North High Street, whose commander for a short time was General Lew Wallace, author of *Ben Hur*. The prosperity of having six thousand men nearby to buy things catapulted the small commercial area into wealth.

One North Columbus woman, Mrs. Catherine Ramlow, made enough money from the war to help create the Great Northern Savings Bank (now a tavern) and the large, ornate Italianate Ramlow Block Building (now a tavern) with her son Peter. Hardworking and business-savvy, she was a long way from her roots as kitchen help in the American House downtown. The taverns and saloons of North Columbus were aided by both the thirsty soldiers and Clintonville laws, which maintained a temperance policy that lasted well into the twentieth century—many taverns would remain watering holes throughout Prohibition.

William Neil, landowner and proprietor of the Neil House, lived where the Main Library of Ohio State now stands. His son, Robert, named his home "Indianola" and platted the street named "Iuka" to be a path to his front door on Fifteenth and Indianola (now the Kappa Sigma Fraternity). Both words were borrowed from Robert's own adventures in Mississippi, where he fought in the Battle of Iuka near Indianola, Mississippi. Robert had the honor of being the first man to enlist for the Union from Ohio.

When the war ended, it ended as it had begun—in churches and saloons, with prayers and toasting. However, within a week, everyone in Columbus knew that by the end of April, Lincoln would be coming through Columbus again. Only this time, it would be for burial in Springfield, Illinois.

The Civil War made Columbus wealthy. The industries of the North had won the war, and now as the victors, Northerners used the factories and railroads, and even the woolen mills and uniform-making factories were poised to create new technologies, communication and consumer markets.

Taverns and saloons were now exclusively in the world of men—well represented by the Elevator Brewing Company, formerly the Bott Brothers Saloon.

The Elevator occupies the southern storefront of the Larrimer Building, designed by Stribling and Lum, which operated as a firm from 1902 to 1933. Larrimer is the commonly recognized name for the building but not the original historic name. The Larrimers purchased the building in the 1960s.

Charles Stribling, the architect, worked with the Fish Stone Company to produce High Victorian Italianate–style buildings, like the Hinman-Beatty Block and Citizens' Savings Bank at 98–104 North High and the Clinton Building at 266 North High. Stribling, born in 1852, was a native of Circleville, Ohio, and originally studied to be a carpenter. He also designed the Brunson Building, at 145 North High; the Union Block, at 131 North High; and the Greene and Joyce Building, at 245 North High.

The Larrimer Building's strong stone façade, even in the nineteenth century, was unusual for its day. Many of its neighbors were brick buildings of three or four stories with arched windows, but the Larrimer had a smooth, yellow sandstone façade and highly ornamented lintels over the main windows. An outside staircase led to the forty billiard tables and other delights upstairs.

When the Larrimer Building was constructed about 1890, one of Columbus's most popular mayors, Mayor George Karb, was just taking office. He would serve three terms, one in the 1890s and two more around World War I. He is a fitting model of the type of man admired in this time period and for the type of saloon patron that the Bott Brothers represented—worldly, magnetic and always quotable. He coined the term "good old Columbus town," which may not seem catchy, but it would live on in James Thurber's writings and was a term that appeared with some regularity even in the *New York Times*.

If Karb was the model man for the culture of the Bott Brothers Saloon, who was he? Karb was the third German mayor of Columbus. He established the police court (for the disturbances of the peace that happened often in taverns and saloons). He shouted, "Good morning, Colonel!" at any passing man on the street. He could speak French and did so when he welcomed French hero Marshall Joffe to Columbus. He would break into Welsh whenever he was near the Welsh church on East Long Street (now Faith Mission). Columbus had a sizeable Welsh population. Karb would sing a popular ditty, "Too Much Mustard," whenever he was in a restaurant.

He was a lot more fun than Mayor Hinkle, a contemporary of Karb's. Hinkle, a soap maker and unheard-of Democrat from Highland Avenue on the North End, once burst into a tent at the Ohio State Fairgrounds and declared, "I am Mayor Hinkle, and I forbid hoochie-koochie dancing here!" Hinkle spent just thirty-five dollars on his entire campaign, proving he was a sort of low-budget guy.

To put the times in perspective, in 1890, when the Larrimer Building was constructed, Columbus son and famous World War I aviator Captain Eddie Rickenbacker was born. Emily Dickenson's first poems had just been printed, and Sitting Bull had been captured. Old North High (later Everett Junior High), old East High (later Franklin Junior High), Fair Avenue and Avondale Elementary Schools were being built. Schoedinger's Funeral Chapel was already open, and the High Street viaduct was still a year or two away from construction (as were Orton Hall and Hayes Hall at Ohio State). Among the sixty-eight thousand residents who lived in Columbus was a ten-year-old, growing up on East Rich Street, who liked to draw pictures for his friends if they fed him candy—George Bellows, the artist who would become synonymous with the Ashcan School of Art. His father, also George Bellows, had already acquired his fame as an architect, notably for the Franklin County Court House across from the Jury Room.

The Bott Brothers' business was originally across from the Ohio Statehouse. They moved into the Larrimer Building's first floor, taking their elaborate curved glass façade to the new location. The storefront

A parade in 1910, with the Special Police Barbecue streetcar in the center, passes the intersection of Long and High. Notice the Bott Brothers building in background. *CML.*

was built about 1898 for brothers Joseph and William to call attention to their billiard and bowling alley and bar supply firm. By 1902, the Bott Brothers had gone into the saloon business and, by 1905, had moved their buffet and billiards to the Larrimer Building when their other building was demolished for a new Mills Restaurant. Many older Columbus residents did not realize the elaborate storefront existed because they never saw it in their lifetime, as it had been covered over by the Clock Restaurant who occupied that space.

The huge and ornately detailed front bar originally came from the 1893 Chicago World's Fair. The electric sign depicted a pool table where the pool cue came down, and the balls scattered. It had been made by the Yoeger Company that made many spectacular pulsating electric bulb signs, including a woman riding a galloping horse for a vaudeville theater on East Gay Street.

The Bott Brothers were ever expanding businessmen—in profit and in girth (portly men were much admired in the Gilded Age). In addition to supplying recreational game tables to Columbus businesses, they sold iceboxes and conveniently owned the Crystal Ice Manufacturing Company and later the Crystal Soda Water Company. They sold "plain and fancy-backed playing cards" and even bathroom fixtures. It was good diversity,

Bott Brothers' extravagant electric sign that was one of the first of its kind in the United States, circa 1900s. *CML*.

as the saloon business could be tricky—Columbus had 340 saloons in the 1890s. Best to establish one's saloon as a an elegant bachelor pad away from home, one that would appeal to lawyers, of whom there were 375 in the city.

Joseph Bott lived at 133 Deshler. Brother William was president of the Bott and Cannon Company that sold wholesale liquor, and he lived at various hotels when he was not courting Mrs. Peter Sells at her home on Goodale Park.

Peter Sells, along with his brothers, owned the Sells Brothers Circus, based in Columbus, with winter headquarters in the unannexed area of Sellsville, on the west side of the Olentangy River (behind Lennox Center). He traveled a great deal but had built an amazing house for his bride on the

Joseph F. Bott came to Columbus in 1876 and co-founded Bott Brothers Saloon in 1886 and Bott and Cannon Wholesale Liquors in 1888. Photo circa 1869. *CML.*

William Bott, brother of Joseph and co-founder of Bott Brothers Saloon. *CML.*

Home of Peter Sells shown in this 1897 photo. William Bott lived nearby. The Sells mansion was later the scene of a sex scandal. *CML.*

northwest corner of Goodale Park. Its style has often been described as High Victorian Circus because it resembled a large and elaborate circus tent.

Lonely, bored and probably a little spoiled, young Mrs. Sells had a small child and a desire to be the object of desire. Flirtation led to indiscretion, and William Bott was seen going to and from the Sells House with no Mr. Sells in sight. Mrs. Sells was seen in the doorway of her home with only her morning wrap loosely covering her when Mr. Bott was in the house. Sells knew which way the wind was blowing when he hired a private detective.

The detective confirmed the appearance of an affair, but luck was on his side when he saw Bott showing off a new fad—the bicycle. Bott placed his bicycle in the Sells bushes, and the detective, hiding behind the Fish Gate (so named because Mr. Fish of Fish Stone Company who lived opposite the Sells donated the gate to the park), scampered across the street to impound the bicycle.

With proof in hand and eyewitness gossips up and down the street ready to testify, Sells won a divorce. Bott remained a bachelor. Mrs. Sells took one of the many well-run trains out of Columbus and did not return.

If scandal touched the personal life of the Botts, another scandal in the saloon has entered into urban legend. Colonel John Rathbone, having a few sips at the back bar, supposedly met his death when an unidentified and, for the most part, unclad woman slipped into the back bar and plunged a dagger into Rathbone's evil heart. Rathbone was a notorious womanizer who plucked his victims of their innocence and left them. The mysterious woman, barefoot and clad in a blanket, disappeared into a snowstorm, leaving Rathbone spitting blood. There was speculation that she had arrived by carriage or had come from the upstairs, where rooms could be rented for private meetings, and had fled toward the river. For many years, a bronze statue of a woman located on the front bar was named "Avenging Fury" in her honor.

As a man's bar, things went on that would not have happened in a respectable mixed-gender establishment. Under the front bar and the bar stools is a slight indentation running the length of the bar. Such troughs carried a trickle of running water that led out the front door and to the street. Just the place to spit one's tobacco (if the spittoon was not convenient), or just spit, or, heck, just relieve one's self. Since men stood at the bar and did not use bar stools, who would notice? Actually, the people on the street passing by who slipped on frozen "stuff" in the winter might take notice. Spitting was recognized as the perfect medium for carrying consumption, and cities, including Columbus, ordered paving bricks that clearly stated "No spitting" for city sidewalks.

Billiards or pool had been a popular sport starting in the nineteenth century; however, many mothers feared this pastime because vice and

Bott Brothers' interior at 161 North High Street circa 1900s, showing billiard tables. Billiards in saloons were suspected of contributing to a decline in morals. *CML*.

temptations were close by. Mrs. Kelton kept a billiards table in her home on East Town Street to keep her children at home. Chic Harley, famed Ohio State football player whose popularity built the Ohio Stadium, was a good pool player and frequently played at Botts in the early twentieth century. Every fraternity house had a pool table, but the pool tables of the big city saloons were more alluring.

In 1919–20, the Larrimer property was owned by George L. and Lena Hoster of Hoster Brewing Company fame. It was rumored that during Prohibition, state legislatures could access the establishment directly from the statehouse basement through underground ventilating tunnels that ran under much of High Street. In the basement of the saloon, alcohol was stored at a perfect temperature for sipping. Later in the 1920s, the old saloon became the Clock Restaurant.

In 1925, the Clock Restaurant was established by Alfred Brenholts and his son, Roy. The name has been erroneously attributed to Earl Doersam, an early manager, but he did not arrive until 1935, and by then, the name was established. Doersam owned other restaurants at 13–15 East Broad and 279 North High. During Prohibition, the Clock advertised malted shakes, soft drinks and sandwiches—and possibly drinks for legislators in the basement. Of course, now there were officially 350 restaurants in downtown and zero saloons.

Amazingly, throughout Columbus, there was a rise in the number of confectionary and candy shops—over 250—during the 1930s. Confectionaries could legally obtain large amounts of sugar, also a necessary ingredient in the fermentation process, and malt was still available for purchase since it was not alcohol. As long as fudge was going out the front door of a house or small shop, who snooped around the back door?

In 1935, the Clock Restaurant had porterhouse steaks for ninety-five cents and Italian spaghetti and bread and butter for twenty-five cents, but it still needed a gimmick of its own. In the same year, the restaurant added a large free-standing street clock in front—one with a cartoon-like face and a place to sit at its base. The clock was a lively and charming fixture downtown, though in November 1969, it was toppled by a windstorm, when it fell through a no-parking standard, smashing the clock beyond repair.

In 1935 and 1941, the property was owned, respectively, by Carl Hoster and George S. Hoster. In 1952, the value of the Larrimer Building was worth almost $190,000; in the 1930s, it had been worth twice as much. In 1945, the Clock was sold to Carl Fisher, who installed a cigar store in the front behind the curved bay windows. From 1954 to 1971, Don Herb was

An early ad for the Clock Restaurant does not mention beer or its past as the Bott Brothers Saloon. *CML.*

the owner. Little had changed. One waitress, Cora Tover, had been there thirty-seven years.

The sixty-five-foot Philippine mahogany bar with mother of pearl inlay stayed intact. Other places that had original mahogany bars were the Jai Lai, Reebs and Deibels, now gone. In the 1960s, the Clock was the oldest continuously operating poolroom in the country and still maintained the distinction of having one of the first intricate electric signs in the country.

Billiards was not the only sport associated with the saloon. In the 1940s and 1950s, Al Haft, the wrestling and boxing promoter, had an office and gymnasium upstairs over the restaurant. Many sports stars of the world gathered there. Wrestling was the top sport of 1950 and was featured on television. Haft ran Haft's Half Track in the Short North. One wrestler who came to visit was Ted Victor—his real name was George Zaharias—and he also came with his wife, one of the greatest female athletes of the twentieth century, Babe Didrikson Zaharias.

When the Clock closed in 1979, there appeared to be few interested in buying it, until Lisa Galat appeared. Galat owned a Matter of Taste on West Fifth Avenue, a restaurant and cooking school, and she learned the art of financing a restaurant through a variety of means, such as the use of blanket mortgages, second mortgages, using twenty-one rental properties for leverage, limited partnerships, long-term leases for historic depreciation, loans from the Small Business Administration and pledges of collateral. In short, she was the consummate businesswoman and had contracts for $650,000 in construction loans with only $525,000 in hand.

Bott Brothers' elegant front bar inside the High Street entrance was made for the 1893 World's Fair in Chicago and still exists today. *CML.*

In the end, with the help of Schooley Caldwell Architects, the cost of restoration in the 1980s was almost $900,000, but when Galat was done, Columbus took notice. It was the first time many had ever seen the lovely original storefront windows or ventured inside. Much of the interior from the Bott Brothers Saloon and the Clock Restaurant went to auction, but the bar remained, and new things were added.

The stained-glass window in the back bar came from a Methodist Church that stood at Twelfth and Indianola Avenues. The windows were executed by Rossbaugh studios—one of several stained-glass studios in nineteenth-century Columbus—and second only to the windows of the Van Gerichten studios. They had been ordered especially for the church, extremely expensive and of the highest quality of materials and workmanship. The large oil painting by contemporary Columbus artist Ron Anderson pictures a billiard room and hangs near antique billiard tables and equipment near the back bar.

Just as the former Bott Brothers Saloon represented the world of the Victorian male, a world of peacocks and puffery and a place where men often addressed each other by the term "Colonel" as if they had all been in the Civil War, another drinking establishment was coming into being to take its place with a focus on both politics and sports.

The Ringside Tavern is only twenty-five feet by thirty-seven feet. From its diminutive architectural scale to its ten-stool bar, and from its small booths and tables to its tiny ladies' room, it a gem to be discovered in Pearl Alley behind the Rhodes Office Tower.

The Ringside's architect was Carl Howell of Howell and Thomas who designed in Columbus from 1908 to 1919. Howell was a native of Columbus who studied architecture at Ohio State University and at the University of Pennsylvania, as well as in Europe. For a time he worked with the well known Yost and Packard firm. In 1908, he joined with another Columbus architect, James Thomas, and their firm was located at 151 East Broad Street.

In addition to the Ringside, the Howell and Thomas team designed other buildings in Columbus, such as the Maramor at 137 East Broad, an elegant supper club and nightclub that brought famous entertainers to town and was torn down in the early 1970s. Buildings that remain include East High School, built in a neoclassical-style in 1922; a home at 2355 Commonwealth Park in Bexley in a Tudor-influenced style in 1926; a Georgian Revival–style

The entrance to today's Ringside Café at 19 North Pearl Street. Little has changed since 1910. *CML.*

100

home in Bexley in 1927 at 311 North Drexel; the Trinity Episcopal Church parish house at Broad and Third; and the Congregational Church (also called the Lincoln Road Chapel in Grandview Heights) that is a mixture of Gothic Revival and Mission-style.

Howell and Thomas also did the Schoedinger and Company Funeral Chapel on East State Street in 1918. Their work was commended by none other than famed architect Howard Dwight Smith, architect of the Ohio Stadium and two Columbus schools, West High School and Indianola Junior High. Smith called their work one of the first buildings in the United States to mix an elegant and modern façade with a stately preexisting building. The funeral chapel's core is a post–Civil War brick house once belonging to Dr. Starling Loving, founder of Starling Medical College, and a relation of the Sullivant family.

Carl Howell was designing both a saloon (the Ringside) and a church building (Trinity's parish house) at the same time. After working in Columbus for a number of years, the firm moved to Cleveland to work with the Van Swearingen brothers to help develop Shaker Heights.

With such an architectural lineage and fluency in building styles, it is interesting to note that the Ringside is a little bohemian Arts and Crafts–style nook. Solid limestone foundation, single-story brick walls and bricks in recessed panels complement the exterior. The shield-shaped motifs on the outside brick pilasters look like they are supporting the cornices. The entrance is angled, electric bulbs frame the doorway and wood doors have original stained glass.

The interior is an intimate atmosphere enhanced by the original bar and paneling in heavy warm oak. The stained-glass windows came from Belgium and are original to the building. Post-Prohibition, the building became known as the Ringside, and the name was enhanced by a dark and smoky reproduction of boxers done by Columbus native and Ashcan School artist George Bellows.

The Ringside was also called the Chamber of Commerce Café for its proximity to the chamber of commerce around the corner—but legend has it that the chamber of commerce, in an era of growing temperance reform, objected to having its name carved over the doorway. Its name was quickly replaced by carved vines and grapes. The chamber's previous name was the board of trade, but the name was changed to reflect the new business spirit. Boards of trade were old-fashioned; chambers of commerce were new.

Built by downtown landowner Mr. Mithoff, whose father had been the one to recognize the Eagle Coffee House as a thing of the past and ordered

Hidden away down Pearl Ally at 19 North Pearl Street, the Ringside Café interior, with original Arts and Crafts stained glass windows, as seen today. *PC.*

it demolished, the Ringside was to replace the Old Board of Trade Saloon, an 1890s saloon destroyed in a fire. The Ringside's location may have also been determined by a peculiar fight going on in downtown Columbus.

High Street property in the early twentieth century was being reappraised at a thousand dollars a foot more than it had been appraised in 1909. Downtown real estate brokers and property owners were trying to cap the taxation at $3,200 dollars a foot, but with little success. The year 1910 was a year of high job loss, recessions, increased food prices, declining municipal services because of falling revenues, rapid new technologies and the fear of terrorists and anarchists. Sound familiar? Eventually the proposed increase ended, short of a taxpayer revolt.

When the Ringside building was built, the first automobiles in Columbus were making their appearance on the streets, the Lazarus store on the northwest corner of Town and High was completed and the Ohio legislature was introducing a bill to outlaw tipping.

In 1911, the Ringside was known as the Little Café and was owned by John Caven, who lived at 22 East Twelfth Street. The building's most immediate neighbors are now skyscrapers, but in 1910, the area had banks, grocery stores, club rooms and a photo-engraving business. The oldest building on Capitol Square, backing up to the Ringside, is the Hayden Building, dating back to the Civil War.

Behind the Ringside on North High was the building recognized by older residents for the Roy's Jewelry sign, an over-the-top display of electric bulbs on steroids from the firm who designed the Bott Brothers' sign. Few recognized that the building was once the original Smith's European Hotel with its oyster bar. The old board of trade/new chamber of commerce

As seen in 1910, a delivery wagon, streetcars and a lone horseless carriage clatter past Smith's European Hotel on East Broad Street. *CML.*

building on Broad Street, which sparked the saloon's name, lost a corner of its 1888 Victorian façade in 1969 in the middle of the night. The old building was quickly hustled out of the way to make way for the Rhodes Office Tower.

Chapter 4

Reformers in Revolt

On the Streets and Behind the Scenes

The Social Evil
Women of questionable character have been prevented from entering
saloons and ladies parlors and from plying their vocation upon the public
streets and from doors and windows of houses occupied by them…All
notorious wine rooms where lewd women visited…have been closed. Scores
of wine rooms of less notorious character have also been closed. Great
difficulty has been encountered however in closing all wine rooms, for the
reason that many women, whose virtue cannot be questioned, also visit
wine rooms, with husbands and friends…The extent of the venereal peril,
as shown by the testimony of physicians is simply appalling…yet not less
than five hundred such women have found it so difficult to ply their trade
in this city, that they have left…and with them have also gone several
hundred "lovers."
—Annual Reports of the Various Departments of the City of Columbus,
Ohio
For the year ending December 31, 1910

The theater, as conducted today, is one of the rottenest institutions outside
of hell…The dance is the moral graveyard of many innocent girls….
Professor Faulkner was a dancing professor in Oakland, California, and
he made $1000 a month out of his classes and he told me that out of one
class there were eight girls (who) became prostitutes as a direct result of
the dance, and he quit it because he saw what the dance was doing right
in Oakland where 200 girls taken at random…there were 163 who were

*therthrough dancing, 20 through drinking, 10 from willful choice, and 7
because poverty and abuse had driven them to it.*
—*Billy Sunday*
Columbus Evening Dispatch , *January 25, 1913*

*When it is legal to serve beer in any government house, it will naturally be
proper to do so for anyone who desires it at the White House...I myself
do not drink anything with alcoholic content, but that is purely as an
individual thing. I should not dream of imposing my own convictions on
other people as long as they live up to the law of our land.*
—*Eleanor Roosevelt,*
White House press conference, 3 April 1933

In 1933, some Columbus residents may have looked at Prohibition's
end as Eleanor Roosevelt did—drinking alcohol was a personal choice,
after all. Her words seem a little tongue-in-cheek when she said that she
"would not dream of imposing my own convictions on other people."
But Prohibition seemed to have been about imposing convictions on
others. Some in Columbus may have remembered the times and the
circumstances differently.

In Columbus in 1910, there had been many things to worry about—
young men in pool halls, women in wine bars and saloons, lewd predatory
men, massage parlors, houses of prostitution and the effect of all this on
children—and alcohol was a major enabler, if not the underlying cause.

The same 1910 city laws that linked saloons and prostitution as twin
social evils also forbade young men under the age of eighteen from entering
poolrooms and ordered a midnight closing of all saloons. In addition, houses
of prostitution near schools and churches had been closed, attempts were
made to regulate massage parlors where "the most degrading and unnatural
practices were carried on" and the Seventh Street District's houses of
prostitution and all saloons were closed (Grant Avenue in the vicinity of the
present Columbus Metropolitan Library). In addition, houses of prostitution
and "assignation" on West Town, West State, West Rich, West Main and
West Mound Streets were closed.

Billy Sunday, the nationally known evangelist who frequently came to
Columbus, always drew crowds packed in tightly night after night in the
tabernacle auditorium on Goodale Avenue and North High Street. He
may not have liked theaters, but he was good theater himself. As a former
baseball player, he often took a classic pitcher's stand at the pulpit, bending

CRIMES.	NO. OF ARRESTS.
Murder	2
Burglary and Grand Larceny	25
Petit Larceny	21
Assault with intent to kill	4
Bigamy	1
Keeping disorderly houses	27
Visiting houses of ill-fame	112
Drunkenness and Disorderly Conduct	1,122
Common Prostitutes	176
Forestalling Markets	19
Vagrancy	43
Total number of arrests	1,552
Amount collected on account of fines and licenses	$3,839 26

Respectfully submitted,

SAMUEL THOMPSON,

City Marshal and Chief of Police.

This crime chart of the City of Columbus's report to City Council in 1905 illustrates the extent to which the city was battling numerous social problems. *CML.*

Policeman chatting at Broad and High. Behind is Smith's European Hotel, 6 North High Street, circa 1900s. *CML.*

down slightly and winding up this arm, yelling, "Take this, for Jesus." And all this talk of the many loose women who gyrated to dance was enough to strike fear into the hearts of some and lust into the loins of those who just liked good theater.

Already, a movement against alcohol had been raging for almost sixty years. In 1836, a group of women attempted to spark a national protest against alcohol by threatening to withhold sex from their husbands if the men drank. In 1876, the first prohibition amendments to the United States Constitution were introduced into Congress but failed to make it out of committee. Now, in the early twentieth century, it seemed sex, drinking and dance were more apt to be seen as the causes rather than the symptoms of society's ills. The issue was, of course, now out in the open and much easier to bring before the public because of advances in communication and technology. And, yes, the average adult American drank seven gallons of alcohol in a year. Still, Billy Sunday was sure only 3.5 percent of all prostitutes were in their chosen profession because of poverty.

For many Columbus residents, alcohol was not a problem. They self-medicated with the local Pe-ru-na patent medicine of Dr. Samuel Hartman. Supposedly a secret concoction of ingredients that came to him in a dream

The Athletic Club of Columbus, founded in 1912, built this six-story building in 1915. It has a lavish second-floor lounge and unique fourth-floor swimming pool (constructed with the same architectural principles of a battleship). The club is celebrating one hundred years in 2012. *CML.*

where an Indian chief appeared to tell him the cure to all illness, Hartman was done in by another connection to Native Americans—Pe-ru-na was banned from Indian reservations by the federal government in 1906 because it had an alcohol content, some say, as high as 27 percent.

Before the scandal of selling alcohol in patent medicine was revealed, however, Hartman had made enough money to build a hotel, finance the Athletics Club's new headquarters, buy downtown prime real estate for the completion of a marble-clad factory to produce the wonder drug and have the largest dairy farm west of the Alleghany Mountains south of Columbus. His son-in-law became the father of testimonial advertising through the use of bogus newspaper stories that claimed, "I can most assuredly say that anybody afflicted with catarrh (the supposed cause of all illnesses) in any form can be cured by taking Pe-ru-na. Mrs. Kliner, Cleveland."

In 1910, Columbus prided itself on being a "progressive" city. The mayor, wealthy industrialists, city planners, religious leaders, ordinary citizens and women (looking to become part of the city's leadership even if they could not vote) looked at the city that was barely one hundred years old and found it wanting.

Chicago architect Daniel Burnham had created the Union Station and the Wyandotte skyscraper for Columbus. Magnificent houses lined East Broad, East Town and East Rich Streets and stretched to the north around Goodale Park, following the streetcar lines up Neil Avenue. The university was becoming a showpiece.

But slums were no longer just tucked behind the Atlas Building, Union Station or the North High buildings that replaced the Old North Graveyard. There were few parks. The ones that existed were sometimes part of a neighborhood that did not want the poor. Dirty children played in street mud. The banks of the Scioto River did not look any cleaner even though the water was undergoing filtration. Women hung laundry from their porches that cantilevered over floating industrial waste and caught the industrial soot of the factories on both sides of the Scioto.

Civic leaders had created a plan in 1908 that hoped for bold changes— parks along the river, the elimination of slums, clean public restrooms on the order of European water closets, the elimination of unsightly electric lines and infrastructure and a magnificent new boulevard that would stretch from the statehouse through old Franklinton.

The Seventh Street District was so notorious for vice and prostitution that law-abiding people on the north of the worst of it that surrounded the Carnegie Library petitioned to have their part of Seventh renamed as Grant

Avenue. One house of ill-repute, the Primo d'Orient, created a catalogue with pictures of its rooms to circulate at the chamber of commerce. James Thurber's mother, who supposedly had enough mirthful DNA for three people, was apparently serious when she signed the petition. President Grant, a Civil War hero, was a much-beloved native son, but it does not seem to have dawned on the residents that he, as an alcoholic, was also the poster child of the problem and therefore not an appropriate namesake.

The temperance movement had gained in strength throughout the nineteenth century, though Americans' consumption of hard liquor had decreased. American beer consumption, on the other hand, had tripled. Excessive drinking was perhaps more rampant in luxury restaurants than it was in the saloons of the immigrant or the workingman.

The German community, as the largest ethnic group in Columbus, had come into its own, three to five generations away from having just arrived. The German business consortium had created the Great Southern Hotel and Southern Theater and the Italianate-embellished business block to the south.

The *Columbus Dispatch* newspaper supported and courted the German community, relating stories of local men who had been heroes in the Franco-Prussian War and the American Civil War, the activities of the many German organizations from the Bismarcks to the Concordia Singing Society, the larger-than-life personalities of the brewers and the social events of individuals in a Sunday newspaper column "In German Circles." Each week, "In German Circles" carried more than fifty notations of births, deaths, visits, engagements, trivia and summer holidays ("Mr. and Mrs. L.S. Hugentugler have returned from their western trip.")

The Irish had done well for themselves, too. Well represented in the funeral business (the term "undertaking" was going out of vogue), the trades and unions, construction, railroads and the scholarly and religious life of Columbus, the Irish had turned their attention to being excellent public servants and elected officials. They stood for democratic and Democratic principles.

In 1907, as the *Columbus Dispatch* was praising the German community, a love-hate relationship seemed to be developing. The newspaper chose to support the temperance efforts, not by attacking the controversies over alcohol consumption, but by attacking the real enemies of morality—Sunday saloon sales and the Brewery Trust that protected and supported the sales.

In September 1907, after weeks of inflammatory articles, which included listing all of the saloons and (especially brewery-owned saloons) that violated Columbus's Sunday closing laws, the *Columbus Dispatch* launched a powerful weapon—a combination of moral authority and wide-eyed

King Gambrinus statue of the August Wagner Brewery at 605 South Front Street, reportedly modeled after August Wagner. The company was in business from 1905 to 1975. The statue was saved and is now displayed in the Brewery District. *CML*.

This *Save the Children* illustration on the front page of the *Columbus Evening Dispatch* on September 11, 1907, was part of an attempt to close saloons on Sunday. *Illustration by Billy Ireland, OSUCL and CD.*

innocence—Reverend Washington Gladden and thousands of Columbus children. Schoolchildren were encouraged to begin a children's crusade against the Sunday saloon sales, signing petitions and marching downtown.

But first, important background history to understanding all the competing interests that formed "the perfect storm" of Prohibition. Pencils ready? There will not be a quiz.

Don't blame the Puritans who held to the thin line between alcohol consumption and excessive alcohol consumption. If they chose to abstain, it was personal, though probably less healthy. They walked into taverns but tried not to stagger out. Prohibition was about power—who has it, who wants it and who (in the eyes of others) deserves it.

The unfortunate gunplay on High and Town Streets that resulted in one man's death during a Fourth of July German parade in 1851 was not an isolated incident. The nativist Know-Nothing Party supporters of the nineteenth century were now just nativist, equal-opportunity haters—anti-Irish, anti-German, anti-Pope and, oh yes, anti-Jew. Many who held nativist feelings probably did not see themselves as any less moral or charitable toward their fellow humans or even knew someone who was different from their small town Lutheran pea-casserole-hot-dish friends. They only read about it in the papers. In the large urban areas, inspired by left-over Whig-Party-I-guess-we-are-Republicans-now attitudes, anti-Democrat Party feelings erupted in riots in New York, Massachusetts and Rhode Island.

Purposely contrived, made-up memoirs inflamed those who believed that Catholics really did hold young women captive in convents (apparently, captivity stories by Native Americans had been a genre of by-gone generations). With no Fox News to report fair and balanced coverage or do fact checking, those who chose (or wanted) to believe took positive steps to solve the matter, burning down convents. Lyman Beecher, father of author Harriet Beecher Stowe and the brilliant but egotistical and slightly adulterous Henry Ward Beecher, made an appearance in Columbus (or the "West," as he called it) at the (now) Central Presbyterian Church. He bought the kidnapped girl story and may have added to its tragic outcomes through his sermons. He was in town to convince the Presbyterians that they really did not want to become Congregationalists who were erring in thinking free will made more sense than predestination (a view his own son, Henry, advocated).

The nativists used religion to justify their beliefs, and this was easy to do because America was in the midst of a Second Great Awakening (some might add "rude"). People were perfectible. Reform was everywhere—rivers, parks, drunks, souls, sins-of-Onan-doers (Onan was a famous masturbator mentioned in the Bible). Taken to extremes, reformers like Sylvester Graham believed a perfect food of grains (his Graham crackers) could cure excesses, including masturbation.

Many in Columbus had Southern roots, and bourbon had watered the roots of those who had come from Kentucky. Others from Pennsylvania held whiskey in high esteem in remembrance of their Whiskey Rebellion, the only time a sitting president of the United States, George Washington, rode into battle, much less against fellow Americans.

"Little Willie's plaint" in the *Columbus Dispatch*, October 30, 1903, illustrates the competing ideologies that surrounded the times prior to Prohibition. *CCJ*.

Alcohol had not caused temperance outbreaks in the South until the end of Reconstruction. And even if Columbus residents did not experience these things firsthand, they had Southern relatives who wrote letters. With citizenship for African Americans, whites viewed alcohol in the hands of person with new rights as worthy of suspicion, fear or hostility.

Already, the backlash of years of enforced Reconstruction laws in the South began with the election of Ohio native Rutherford B. Hayes as president of the United States and the removal of troops enforcing Reconstruction ordinances. Hayes's wife, Lucy, had carried her own temperance movement into the White House as a personal decision. However, by the election of President Woodrow Wilson (the grandfather for whom he was named is buried in Green Lawn Cemetery), racism in the South made temperance a good option (at least for the other fellow).

Racism was heightened both in the North and South by the new technology of the times—the silent movie. *Birth of a Nation* helped to create the myth of the Lost Cause and cast the Ku Klux Klan as the champions of Southern women's virtue. It was Wilson's favorite movie. It was shown almost continuously in the White House for members of Congress and routinely played in cities for free. To be charitable, perhaps Wilson accepted the false premises of the movie because the novels of captive girls in Catholic convents were not available in the White House library.

Pencils down. Quick recap—Columbus women in wine bars, Grant Avenue, 1908 Plan, Lyman Beecher, Graham Crackers, masturbation, bourbon, Lemonade Lucy, Reconstruction, captive girls in Catholic convents.

They all connect to Columbus's historic taverns and saloons—Irish and Germans, blue laws and breweries, Milo Grogan, Westerville, Ohio, a scary boy automaton yet to make his appearance and, oh yes, Reverend Washington Gladden, the *Columbus Dispatch* and thousands of Columbus children.

Irish and German workingmen had only one day off in the week—Sunday. After Mass at St. Patrick's or St. Mary's, this was quality time. Sunday was for socializing, sports, family and drinking. Germans looked forward to a beer garden outing that included the whole family and possibly even one where singing societies or classical music could be heard.

The Irish, too, gathered with friends and family for conversation and music. Others, going home to the traditionally quiet and reverent Sunday afternoon, found this an offensive sight. Not only did many believe that the Irish, along with the Germans, had a monopoly on the alcohol production in the country, but here they were laughing, enjoying the bonding of community and plotting Democrat takeovers (saloon politics). People in Columbus read papers; they had heard of the mine strikes. Wherever the Irish went, labor

St. Patrick's Roman Catholic Church (dedicated in 1853), as seen in this 1891 photo, was the heart of the Irish community. *CML.*

troubles and plots followed. There were documented anarchists in Chicago with ties to French Communards and German socialists.

In 1901, President William McKinley was assassinated by Leon Czolgosz, who had no political associations but a foreign surname, and he had been living in a Buffalo, New York hotel/tavern for three days prior to his deed. Connections were made to a previous assassination in 1881, when President James Garfield had been shot by Charles Guiteau, a moderate drinker, who supposedly used a stiff drink for courage before his action. Rumor suggested that anarchists toasted Czolgosz at the same time the news of the shooting was just reaching across the country.

Secret service agents, concerned and aggressive, led a raid on a Polish saloon in Oregon, where secret plans for anarchy were found. Once

From Now On. Prohibition has arrived in Ohio and the United States. *Illustration by Billy Ireland, OSUCL and CD.*

116

translated, the secret plans turned out to be notes for the building of a church.

Temperance reform for alcohol came with differences. There were direct action campaigns like Carrie Nation's in Hillsborro, Ohio. Nation might bravely march into a saloon with her hatchet to smash bottles and hope that she was not attacked in return, but the majority of direct action campaigns in Ohio and elsewhere were women (and very brave men) who kept vigil outside saloons, singing and praying that those who drank away their paychecks and starved their children would have a change of heart. Starving children, beaten wives and slum conditions were both very real and very much used as propaganda.

The Women's Christian Temperance Union (the WCTU) had an impact, though some saloons might only close for a few days and reopen, or take delight in verbally abusing the reformers or giving them a baptism of icy or scalding water. Supposedly Mrs. Wagner, female saloon owner of the Holly Tree Coffee and Lunch Rooms, in Columbus, nearly chocked a reformer to death. The WCTU had a headquarters on East Broad Street that, in the 1980s, still had a houseful of literature and other promotional materials.

In addition to being anti-alcohol, the WCTU was ahead of the times in calling attention to the dangers of smoking (which it saw as closely aligned with alcohol consumption). One device it used was an automaton, a mechanical full-scale bust of a boy behind a podium. When manually wound, his eyes lighted, his mechanical hand turned pages in a book on the podium and he would begin to "read" about the dangers of smoking. He had been created for use at the Ohio State Fairs, a gimmick to draw in young listeners (or give them nightmares).

The WCTU was effective and well known. There were other reformers, but none as powerful or savvy as the one in Columbus's backyard—Westerville's Anti-Saloon League. They created pressure politics because they were nonpartisan, well organized and pumped out volumes of literature—including accurate statistics and the impact of alcohol in other countries (including sacramental wine). Westerville's post office was created to handle the mail generated by the Anti-Saloon League. In 1890, an estimated two hundred people were employed to produce over 250 million pages of material each month.

Shrewd leadership in the Anti-Saloon League kept the message simple and digestible—all saloons were bad. Songs, plays, short stories, posters, flyers and their own encyclopedia repeated the message. Industrial moguls like John D. Rockefeller, Henry Ford and Pierre du Pont believed the message. Without alcohol, their workers would be more productive; without saloons, the chance of unions and strikes would lessen. By the 1920s, Rockefeller stopped giving money, and du Pont did a complete about-face on his convictions. Both not only saw the rise of organized crime that supplied illegal liquor, but du Pont especially saw the corruption of young women in the seductive nature of forbidden pleasures. Ford did not change his mind.

In Columbus, the clear message was compounded by the fact that the very devil lived in the South Side. It did not matter that the brewery industry employed thousands whose jobs depended on the making of beer—the barrel makers, stable hands, distributors, salesmen, laborers, drivers or craftsmen—nor that breweries supported churches, recreation for children and sports teams or that the money kept Columbus's railroads, construction, banks and other industries supported or that the breweries were firmly embedded in Columbus's culture, dating from before the Civil War.

Louis Hoster had arrived in 1835. George Schlegel was part of a brewery in 1850. Nicholas Schlee, Schlegel's nephew, returned to Germany in 1856,

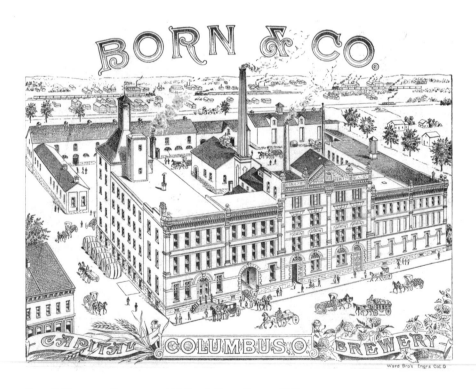

Born & Company Brewery at 449 South Front Street. *CML.*

the year his uncle died of typhoid, to learn brew making and improve the Columbus product. Conrad Born had arrived in 1834 as a butcher and entered into partnerships to make the new lighter lager beers, and he left as the creator of the modern industry. Along the way, he sponsored relatives and employees to become entrepreneurs.

The Hosters, Schlegels, Borns, Silbernagles, Schlees, Wagners, Moerleins, Zimmermans and the Blenkers were partners in marriages, community events or businesses, and their lives were deeper than the tunnel that ran underneath Front Street from the Schlee Brewery to the family home (Germania). The breweries include Franklin Brewery, City Brewery, Gambrinus Brewery, Washington Brewery and Born Brewery. There were partnership industries, including: the Born and Schlee Bavarian Brewery; Schlegel and Blenker Bavarian Brewery; the City Park Brewery; and the Born, Schlee and Hoster Brewery.

The breweries in Columbus and elsewhere began to exercise good business practices, investments and ways to keep costs down and profits up using a technique common among Carnegie, Ford and Rockefeller—vertical alignment. By setting up saloons and taverns as part of their network, the product could be expanded by buying buildings and providing tavern owners

Corner of South High and Mound Streets, the Grand Army of Republic Band and the National Encampment marches past the Frech Brothers Restaurant and Saloon, as seen in 1888. *CML.*

with everything they needed, barware included. What was an acceptable practice in steel, coal or railroads was labeled as the "brewery trust" by the *Columbus Dispatch*. The Hoster Brewery purchased many saloons in order to market their beer.

By targeting the trust and promoting the leadership of Reverend Washington Gladden, rather than suggesting immigrants were less loyal or alienating the solid German citizens, the newspaper could accomplish several goals—increased readership, being on the right side of the new morality and solving other civic issues like tax bases and needed infrastructure improvements, ironically needed most in the South Side.

Who was suggesting eliminating all drinking? Who would want to put thousands out of work and lose that tax base? This was about drinking on Sunday.

Sunday closing laws, the so-called local blue laws, were in every major city and small town in America, and, for the most part, there still are restricted hours for some businesses on the Christian Sabbath. Blue laws may have referred to the blue paper on which New England laws were written in the seventeenth century, or they may have reflected a patriotic sentiment of being "true blue" to certain sacred principles. Regardless,

Pictured in 1909 at 347 East Mound, Mendel Trope operated the saloon on the right (notice the free soup sign) and a grocery on the left. *CML.*

for many it was less about religion than it was about immigrants (yes, still hating those immigrants—old ones, new ones, red ones, blue ones).

Others have suggested it was a power play between the old Anglo-Saxon businessmen and what they perceived to be the threat of the immigrants. But the Germans were already part of the powerful business interests in retail, manufacturing, industry, publishing and transportation. The ward system for electing city officials actually contained the German influence on one end of town as it did for the Irish on the other. If new changes to local politics in home rule would lead to a smaller number of city council members from across the city, it would be an advantage to the Irish, who were heavily invested in the political machines of local politics.

Reform for open, clean government was part of the agenda for a progressive society. There were more mundane problems than an anti-Sunday sales agenda could solve.

Gladden was the minister of the First Congregationalist Church in Columbus, ironically composed of the congregation who did not listen to Lyman Beecher's admonitions to stay Presbyterian. Exceedingly well respected across many denominations, Gladden was the ideal civic crusader: a prolific writer and nationally known, having formulated the progressive

Washington Gladden (1836–1918) was minister of First Congregational Church and also served on city council for a short time. He was known nationally for his social reform movement to aid the unfortunate. *CML.*

and reform movements underpinnings with his Social Gospel Movement. Beginning in the 1880s, the Social Gospel movement married good works with salvation. Faith was paramount, but one should work to solve injustices. Gladden was continually leading the fight against the Badlands and for true civic reform—education, slum clearance, parks and water treatment.

On Sunday, September 11, 1907, after days of quenching the thirst of the public for inflamed rhetoric with escalating headlines each day heading up to Sunday, the *Columbus Dispatch* launched the children's crusade against the Sunday saloon. For days before and continuing through Sunday, children's signatures were solicited on a petition (and each scrawl published in its own handwriting) calling for the closure of Sunday saloons. As the *Columbus Dispatch* commented, "There is no cause for comment—the vast fields of characteristic signatures, and the hundreds that could not be reproduced in 'fac-simile,' tells its own story and points to its own tremendous moral."

The city seemed to be on the verge of a civic crisis because of alcohol. As the city tried to crack down on Sunday sales, temperance leagues like the Anti-Saloon League of Ohio and the Brewers' Vigilance Bureau demanded controls on the German beer manufacturers and the many saloons in the city. Especially annoying to the temperance-minded were the places outside the city limits and the German's South Side societies that frequently ignored the city's ordinances. Owners and bartenders on West State and South Fourth Streets, however, were not so lucky. They and many others were arrested on Sunday and charged twenty-five dollars each. Saloons in Hanford Village, near Livingston Avenue and Nelson Road, were not checked because the Columbus chief of police thought they were annexed into Columbus, though they had not been.

But as some saloons started to comply with the pressure of closing on Sunday, township saloons did "a land office business without molestation." A saloon on South High in Marion Township, along with others, was said to have the biggest day turnout in years on a Sunday.

"I am tickled to death to get to keep my restaurant open," said one High Street saloonkeeper in the city. The mayor had ordered that the barroom at the back must be sealed off on Sundays in an attempt to maintain control of the situation. Wayne Wheeler himself, of the Westerville's Anti-Saloon League, and Gail Hartley, official spokesperson for the Brewers' Vigilance Bureau, inspected Sunday establishments together. Both pronounced their inspection as a good trial run since the following Sunday, the police were being instructed to make arrests for owners and patrons alike who violated the new rules.

The Capital City's Most Storied Saloons

Already there were rumors of violations at the Capital Tavern that was said to have been doing some "bootlegging" during the day, selling half pint bottles at fifty cents each to the thirsty in the vicinity of State and High and Town and High. Also, "women of questionable character who parade the streets were conspicuous by their presence," and one, Ruth Smith, age twenty, was arrested shortly after midnight on Saturday for being on the street. She was given a fine of twenty-five dollars and costs in police court on Monday morning.

Closing Sunday saloon sales was important, but outside the city, there were many places to drink. If a person did not belong to a private society like the Maennerchor, one could simply drive to the nearest spot outside of the city limits. In 1910, Mayor Marshall warned the citizens of Columbus against going into the township saloons on Sunday and becoming intoxicated, and he warned the townships that they had a responsibility to regulate their saloons. "You will close them on Sunday, also, in order to protect our citizens, notwithstanding the fact that they are located beyond the corporation limits." He had notified the chief of police that if Columbus citizens arrived home intoxicated, the "jags" would come in. The warning may have had an effect. A new saloon on the outskirts of the city on St. Clair Avenue closed a month later, though business was flourishing on Sundays. John Griffin, the bartender, reported that his boss Michael Cahill had suddenly departed, leaving a note to pay his bills and close up, saying he was "disgusted" and had left for California where he had relatives.

Milo Grogan had started off as two rural communities just past Fort Hayes on Cleveland Avenue. Milo was platted and lots sold, starting in 1888, by Jonathan Fallis Linton, who had developed other Columbus subdivisions. In 1894, John Patrick Grogan opened a grocery and dry goods store at 1355 Cleveland Avenue. The community centered on the activities they shared near the railroad tracks. Both Milo and Grogan each had a post office and were considered separate communities.

Milo stretched along Cleveland Avenue from First to Fifth Avenues. Grogan was west of Cleveland Avenue and ran northwest to the Ohio State fairgrounds at Eleventh Avenue. They shared a business community along Cleveland Avenue, a school, occupations associated with the railroads and, generally, the Catholic faith. There were many Irish and Italians, many boardinghouses for workers and many saloons.

That the area could be a little rowdy was an understatement. In the Italian saloons, there were fears that the Black Hand, the forerunner of what is commonly called the Mafia, was already there—perhaps not so much among all of citizens of Columbus, but certainly among the Italians who lived there. Two months before Gladden addressed the children of Columbus, the Black Hand was suspected in the shooting of detective Frederick Laage of Milo. Laage had been ambushed. Two days before that incident, an Italian immigrant was found dead in the nearby bushes. Wondering newspapers tried to link it to other events, including a murder in a Milo saloon, and published explanations of "murder societies" among immigrant groups, ending with the phrase most often heard on Columbus's news stations today—"Can it happen here?"

According to the late Ben Hayes, historian and columnist for the *Citizen Journal*, Milo could be a little wild, and the "wild" boarders were directed to a boardinghouse unofficially known as the Blue Lodge of Profanity.

The landmarks of the community would, in time, center on a circus grounds, the Timken Company, St. Peters Catholic Church, the Milo Elementary School and the Columbus Railway Power and Light Company station, as well as the commerce associated with the barracks at Fort Hayes.

In the same years of the anti-saloon movement, Milo had been deciding, since the 1890s, whether or not it wanted to be an independent village. The City of Columbus was nudging them to come into the city—they would not only increase the tax base for Columbus but would also end the pesky problem of getting a convenient Sunday drink. The communities sat along the Panhandle railroad, and shops and industry were beginning to be pushed off of the high-priced downtown land and were moving either north or south. One day, the industries that would come to dominate the community would all be paying taxes to Columbus—and just in time, to increase the revenue needed for sewers in the South Side.

Milo residents, beer or wine glass in hand in their taverns, weighed out the arguments before them—annexation to Columbus and get light and water with Columbus? Be independent and pay for basics at a higher price and have to increase their own taxes by one mill?

Now, after ten years of thinking about it in Milo, the *Dispatch* did its part, publicizing a "rousing meeting in the mayor's office" and the advantages for a "Greater Columbus" and stating that "leading citizens of suburbs seek information and lend enthusiasm." Milo and Grogan eventually came into Columbus, aided by political cartoons from popular *Dispatch* cartoonist Billy Ireland.

Problems solved: Milo Grogan gets water and light, Columbus gets taxes, Germans in the South Side get new sewers, the children of Columbus become young activists, Reverend Gladden has a moral victory for the city,

Take Down the Fences was aimed at admitting troublesome Milo Grogan though it was portrayed as increasing the tax base for Columbus. *Illustration by Billy Ireland, OSUCL and CD.*

evil saloon keepers in the clutch of the brewery trust's grasp are shamed, the *Columbus Dispatch* sells papers and—wait, what about that beer on Sunday? Not in Milo Grogan anymore.

So why didn't the issue just stop at Sunday sales? The Anti-Saloon League continued to be the most powerful lobby group of all time, and they were not interested in Sunday sales—the tavern, the saloon, the bar and the dive all had to go. Liquor was the single cause of the problem. The argument was simple, nonsectarian and nonreligious. With the passage of the Volstead Act in 1919, Sunday sales of alcohol were moot, and other issues were rapidly changing attitudes—either in favor of or in opposition to what alcohol meant in society.

Hotels, where anything might happen behind closed doors, coupled with women's new personal freedoms in dress, hairstyles and use of tobacco, threatened middle-class values. Then there was the automobile, a possible substitute for the hotel, which took young people away from protective eyes.

Whenever change is rapid and revolutionary, only two directions seem to be apparent—be it the modernist who embraces the change and flies toward it or be it the traditionalist who hopes it will soon pass. The prohibition of alcohol was only part of the response to rapid changes in communication and technology—it was visible to those who saw the effects of alcohol abuse staggering to the streets from saloons; it was understandable to many who experienced its excesses in their families; it was imagined by those who judged others in slums and settlement houses; and it was a red herring used by politicians and policy makers from the national to the local level who knew which way to court voters.

The excesses of lavish drinking and dining (and oyster bars) also were in hurtful contrast to the images of the young men dying in muddy trenches in France in World War I. Free-flowing liquor was no longer publically tolerated.

With the Volstead Act, there was a general level of acceptance in Columbus, at first. The saloons, taverns, hotels and private clubs each adjusted in their own way.

The Germans responded by making what they called "vinegar" at home. That it looked like beer and smelled like beer did not matter, as long as it was labeled correctly. The Maennerchor responded by listening more closely for its telephone to ring. Someone in the city administration who knew the comings and goings of the police department often tipped off the singing society if it was about to be checked for the sale of alcoholic beverages (one could have them, just not drink them). Some indicated it might be the friendly work of City Councilman Zimpher, a member of the club and a resident of the area. Others remember that Charlie Thurber, James Thurber's father, was a quiet bureaucrat working for the mayor at the time.

During Prohibition, the sixteenth Saengerfest (singing festival) was voted to be held in Columbus in 1931, and other singing groups from Ohio would arrive for the festivities. The Maennerchor needed to enlarge and beautify the home—an auditorium was added and a rathskeller was built—and Germania and others helped to cover the expenses of construction. During this renovation and expansion, the German decorations reminiscent of a German beer hall were added, perhaps in celebration that Prohibition would soon be over—that was what a variety of newspapers across Ohio were predicting. Or they knew they just had to make more vinegar. Various plaques and shields represent a portion of those 250 German cities and principalities from which German-speaking people emigrated.

North of the downtown, during Prohibition, the Higgins Saloon (the Flatiron) was listed as a nameless restaurant on one side and the May Association Store Offices on the other side. The May Company, a retail department store, was nearby. The nameless restaurant may not have done much business and was probably vacant for much of the time. In the intervening years, the saloon portion of the building has been Higgins, Flannigans, Jillians and the Cat's Meow, one of the oldest of the Columbus gay bars, managed by Ernie Toadvine in the 1970s. At various time, owners lived upstairs or had rooms for rent.

After Prohibition, the saloon in which the Main Bar conducted business was often vacant except for an occasional boarder. In the 1940s, there were four apartments upstairs. The single men who rented in the neighborhood were cab drivers or poultry dressers for the old Central Market. Widows also sought the furnished rooms. On the corner of Front and Main, a shoe manufacturer operated in a building that is now self-storage. Nearby was a small Chinese community of businessmen—the Chinese Merchants Association, the Yee Moo Kai Association, the Len Chong Importers, the Hink Fook Company of Oriental Foods, the Chinese Relief Association and two Chinese restaurants, as well as a Chinese wholesale tobacco warehouse. A Russian restaurant and a barber college run by Mr. Kelley, an Irishman, were also nearby.

For the Jury Room, change began even before Prohibition. At the turn of the twentieth century, Emil Hess owned the business and lived on the premises, but by 1911, Hess sold the business to Christian Welde. Welde renamed the business the Welde Café just before Prohibition. He, too, lived in the building, and the name simply became the Café.

Welde continued to own the building and the business through the 1920s, when it served soft drinks. In the decade preceding Prohibition, the building was also leased to the Hoster Brewing Company, part of the wicked beer trust when many of the German breweries directly owned or leased saloons. In the 1930s, the building was owned by Florian Ziegler and remained in the Florian and Raymond Ziegler trust until the 1970s, although the business was owned by many others over the years. In the 1930s through the 1940s, it was known as Irvin's Place, owned by Harry McKay, who lived above the business, and it was still listed as a restaurant although it probably also served alcohol. Harry McKay, in the 1950s, became one of the owners of the Ringside Tavern in Pearl Alley. Welde appears to have given up the saloon business, becoming a laborer and buying a house in the emerging but rural area of Linden, outside of the city limits and in the farmlands and orchards of Cleveland Avenue.

The Jury Room, as it has been known by most Columbus residents, was briefly known as the Grilll (yes, multiple letters), and it has both true tales and yet-to-be resolved urban legends. In the 1950s, two lawyers in a card game reportedly had a gun battle in the bar (shades of early taverns), and one died.

In the 1970s, the Jury Room was the traditional home of the four-hundred-pound sacred Blarney Stone of Columbus's Shamrock Club. Kept in front of a refrigerator in the small kitchen, it had to be wrestled, tugged or continuously rolled aside when the cooler needed restocking. In the 1970s, one of the first signs of spring in downtown Columbus was a balsa wood glider contest, inspired and organized by courthouse workers. From the top of the courthouse, gliders rained down on the Jury Room as each contestant tried to land their glider on its roof. And then there are the ghosts that move objects and the orbs in the basement. That is a different book (and a Columbus Landmarks Foundation October tour).

With the Volstead Act's enforcement, the present-day Ringside had the most amazing transformation, becoming the Jolly Gargoyle and advertising itself as being "down the alley by the Chamber of Commerce." It was run by Mildred Dickey, who lived at 41 East Sixteenth Avenue. Lunches were fifty cents, and it was open "late." It also had competition in the downtown from the Clock, which advertised velvet malted milk and toasted sandwiches. Also serving food late were Staub's Hungarian Dining Room on East Town; Jacque's Bohemian Restaurant on East Broad, which billed itself as the Greenwich Village of Columbus; and the Nookery on North High. The Matsonia Barbeque on West Broad advertised "good music while you dined and "good things to eat, which are delightfully different." The Jolly Gargoyle also had a gift and antique shop that featured "works of art." It was frequented by Hollywood artists and visiting movie stars who regularly purchased gifts when they were in town. Joan Crawford was one customer who stopped there and also at the Maramor (designed by the same architect as the Jolly Gargoyle, remember?).

Every March 6th, the Jolly Gargoyle Tea Room had a birthday party for itself and offered a small token of appreciation to its customers—having their fortunes read free of charge by Ab-d-da-bar in "his den." The Jolly

Logo of the Jolly Gargoyle Art Shop and Tea Room, opened in 1920, soon after Prohibition began. They sold food as well as antiques, books, stationery and novelties. *CML.*

Gargoyle also had a country home, the Tabard, at 4040 Scioto River Road, north of Lane Avenue, that opened seasonally in the summer. In the 1940s, it resumed as a tavern, and the gargoyle flew away.

In the 1960s, the Ringside was owned by Clem Amorose, who had a thirty-year reign in the tavern business. He died in 1992. He had been a veteran of World War II, a member of the Shamrock Club and the ever-jovial and popular host of his establishments. He was a heavy man who always had a cigar in hand, and he was famously quoted as having pronounced his intentions for the Ringside as "a man's type of bar, the kind of pub you see on a corner in New York City." He wanted the ten-stool bar to be like

New York's Stagedoor Deli, and it was said that it was just that with Clem's specialties of meatloaf and hamburgers.

When seven hundred daily newspapers across the country held a straw poll on Prohibition, they did not assume it was right or wrong. There were three choices to mark off on the newspaper ballot to send it—in favor of continuing present Prohibition laws, in favor of modification of Prohibition laws to permit beer and light wines or in favor of complete repeal of Prohibition laws. The results among Columbus, Cleveland, Toledo, Akron and Cincinnati were almost nine times higher for modification or repeal than for keeping Prohibition the same. What is most interesting is that more people wanted the laws modified than repealed. Perhaps they had become used to the malt mixtures they could make at home; others swore their near beers were so tasty, they could not tell the difference.

It would be many more years before it was repealed. Prohibition was successful—alcohol consumption did drop. No one advertised speakeasies in the newspaper, so there is no way to calculate how many there were. It is easier to establish individual cases where drinking just went under cover.

One local spot was the Hey-Hey Bar and Grill on Whittier Street. Because it was located on a major streetcar line, close to Parsons Avenue and the Irish, Hungarians, Croatians and others who worked in the steel mill, glue factories and other industries, the Hey-Hey drew working-class men and women.

Whittier had once been named Schiller Street before World War I. During the war, very German names sometimes changed—probably less imposed on the German community by others than self-imposed by the German Americans to show that they fit in. One poet was traded for another—Frederick Schiller was out, and John Greenleaf Whittier was in.

The street retains the mixed urban fabric that is now gone from many other streets in Columbus—homes, bars, retail, movie theaters and churches all exist together like a variety of village houses under the Christmas tree. Barcelona was the Parkmore Pharmacy. Four benevolent Catholic groups (the 4 S Club) are housed in the old Columbia movie theater that was built by the Steelton Corporation. Steelton was a commonly used name for the South Side below Whittier and near the factories.

Where the Giant Eagle now stands is a marker to the first Ohio State football game that was played there and is a reminder that this was a large field and recreation area popularly known as "the Reckie," short for recreation area. But that was after an Evangelical Temple was built on the site in the 1920s.

The Capital City's Most Storied Saloons

Not many know that Columbus had at least three major Appalachian migrations, most came up Route 23 through the South Side, One was following World War I, and with them, the new migrants, white and black, brought Bible-based gospel religion, fiercely independent ways, and different music.

The Hey-Hey is a good example on the exterior of an Italianate commercial building—and though documents might put the building as 1900, the style implies a building twenty years older. The building's colorful history is associated with Prohibition. Prior to that, August Wagner, the king of the brewers in Columbus who was said to have been the model for his King Gambrinus beer, purchased this bar and seven others. Hosters also purchased bars.

The breweries sold only their brand in the bar but helped to furnish it and provide colorful advertising signs and barware. Small children, even past World War II and into the 1950s, carried home the draft suds for parents.

Wagner appears to have purchased the bar on Whittier in 1914, and he later called it a dry goods and cigar store when liquor sales became illegal. He was one of the most active opponents of the *Columbus Dispatch* and the anti-Sunday saloon sales act. The present-day kitchen was once part of three rooms where card playing took place.

During Prohibition, the outside windows of the bar were covered over. Beer (or "vinegar") was still being made in the neighborhood, illegally, and smuggled to a barn behind the saloon. When it was safe, someone

The Hey-Hey Bar and Grill, located at 361 East Whittier Street, is known for its sauerkraut balls and its unusual name dating from Prohibition. *SB.*

would knock on the door and whisper, "Hey, hey, the beer is here." Hence the name was born. One former owner of the saloon was Charley Hill, a bootlegger, who became known for his Hill's Distributing Company and his racetrack ownerships.

Sue and Tim Gall have owned the business and building since 1981 and say that it had the first beer garden in the city—the area is now for horseshoe playing.

In April 1933, Prohibition had been repealed. What came in with a sigh went out with a bang. Columbus counted down the days, and newspaper pages were filled with advertisements and suggestions for how to celebrate. Unfortunately, the new federal income taxes put into place to help off-set declining revenues from the losses on liquor taxes never went away (yes, the government had thought this out before the Volstead Act went into effect).

Left: Counting down the days until the end of Prohibition, bartender Fritz Beckwith looks to April 7, 1933. *OSJ.*

Opposite page: A 1933 Atlantic & Pacific ad announcing that they now carry beer. *CML.*

For your convenience the A & P Food Stores at the addresses listed below now handle---

BEER

Blatz Brand

6 *12-Ounce Bottles* **75¢**

(Plus 15c Bottle Deposit on Six Bottles)

May not be drunk on the premises. Minimum sale—six bottles to a customer. Maximum sale—48 bottles to a customer. Deposit of 40c required on each wooden case taken from the stores.

Beer now on sale in following stores---

70 East Main Street	3522 North High St.
208 South 4th St.	2586 North High St.
15 West Spring St.	1127 North High St.
1042 Mount Vernon Ave.	2481 Cleveland Ave.
1254 West Broad St.	1563 North 4th St.

THE GREAT **ATLANTIC & PACIFIC** TEA CO.

DOWNTOWN	NORTH	EAST

DOWNTOWN

FOR THAT

Cold Bottle of Beer
and Sandwich

Stop at

The Rex Billiard Parlor

274 N. High St.

We Are Serving
"AUGUSTINER"
15c a Bottle.
"BLATZ" 20c a Bottle.
"PRIMA" 20c a Bottle.
"ATLAS" 20c a Bottle.
"BUDWEISER" 20c a Bottle.

THE CLOCK
161 N. High St.

In the Heart of the City

You Can Drink Your Beer or Buy It and Take it Home.

Try Our Food.

Malted Milk Shop
38 W. Broad St.

NAPPI'S RESTAURANT
17 N. 4TH.
BUDWEISER
BLUE RIBBON
PABST
BLATZ
AUGUSTINER
Best Meals in city, 15c to 35c.

The "KAISERHOFF" Again
Is Here
Serving Good Meals and Ice Cold Beer.
Private Dining Rooms.
Special Luncheons and Dinners.
Just a Few Doors W. of High.
35 W. Gay St.

HARRY M. MERZ
433 S. HIGH

After Pabst, Augustiner and other Beers. Come in and enjoy a bottle or glass of beer with us.

6 Bottles Augustiner
75c

NORTH

BEER—BEER
Take It Home With You or Buy and Drink It Here.

HENNICKS
At the Gate of the Campus.
Enjoy Our Food.
Meals or a la Carte Service.

Beer 15c Per Bottle
Special Lunches and Dinners
25c—30c—35c

T-Bone Steak, 45c
a la Carte Orders.

Parkers Soda Grill
895 N. High St.   UN. 0682

Enjoy a bottle of good beer with our well-prepared home cooking. You'll feel better.

C. & G. Restaurant
1579 N. High St.

Chas. Sourles, Mgr.

BAMBOO INN
Features
Plate Lunches, 25c
Plate Dinners, 30c-50c

Beer 15c Bottle
1990 N. High, So. of 18th Ave.
UN. 0185

Special Plate Lunch
BOTTLE BEER
Swiss Cheese Sandwich
Potato Salad
Baked Beans   **35c**

SPECIAL LUNCHEONS AND
DINNERS

MARY'S LUNCH
OPEN TILL 3 A. M.

EAST

Use Beer as a Beverage

With Chinese Food.
It's Excellent!

GOLDEN LOTUS
Chinese and American
Restaurant
747 E. Broad St.   AD. 006?

Townley Court Dining Room
580 E. TOWN ST.
Has Opened a
"Beer Annex"
Chicken Dinners and Sandwiches
a Specialty.
Parties Given Individual Attention.
Plenty of Parking Space.
AD. 6291.

We Sell and Serve Beer.
Eat a delicious sandwich of our spiced Beef, Corned Beef, Tongue or other Kosher meats with a bottle of Beer; take some home to serve your guests with Beer.

Imported and Domestic
Delicacies of All Kinds.
OPEN TILL MIDNIGHT

HEPPS KOSHER DELICATESSEN
611 E. MAIN ST.   AD. 13?

The
Willard Restaurant
2270 E. Main St.
Now Serves
ATLAS, BUDWEISER & GAMBRINUS

BEER
Steak and Chicken Dinner
OUR SPECIALTY.
FA. 6117.

Beer! Beer! Beer!
Our Soups and Sandwiches
Are Delicious!

Our Beer Ice Cold!
Try Some!
We Will Deliver from Whittier to Broad and High to Alum Creek

H. P. Knisely

"We Serve Beer" directory in a 1933 Ohio State Journal newspaper. *CML.*

A March 31, 1933 cartoon. Prohibition ends and celebration begins—or so many thought. *OSJ.*

Construction worker William O'Grady enjoys a newly legal brew with his noon meal, high above Columbus. *OSJ.*

In 1938, with the Depression fading and war coming, it was announced by E.N. Dietrich, state director of education, that all schools in Columbus would observe Temperance Day on January 14. In an announcement that eerily reflects educational pronouncements made in 2012 (when there were good intentions but little money): "So far as possible, the temperance theme will be tied in with ordinary classroom work...Reading material, composition of essays, social science classes and science classes will deal with temperance and liquor. Repeal of the Eighteenth Amendment has not solved the liquor problem...it has cleared the decks for a new approach," according to George Roudenbush, superintendent of Columbus schools.

Life went on.

Chapter 5
Tavern Spirits

Migratory Souls and Historic Saloons that Never Were

On a corner, a glass-fronted building shed a yellow glare upon the pavements. The open mouth of a saloon called seductively to passengers to enter and annihilate sorrow or create rage.
—*Stephen Crane*
Maggie, Girl of the Streets, *1893*

Do not allow your children to mix drinks. It is unseemly and they use too much vermouth.
—*Fran Leibowitz*
Parental Guidance, *1991*

Poor Maggie, a girl fallen on hard times. A beckoning glow from the saloon—warmth and a drink, a promise to soothe or enrage. What will she do? Stephen Crane liked to present moral dilemmas to his characters because he believed in free will.

For two hundred years or more, the drinking establishments in Columbus have been the places where stories, dilemmas and challenges to free will have happened. There were so many taverns and saloons two hundred years ago that it is not surprising that the history of a present-day tavern turns up two or three more. It is as if the spirit of a former tavern has reclaimed its body. In other cases, there may be spirits other than alcohol that are in the bones of the buildings.

The Char-Bar, Barley's and Mac's in the Short North belong in one category. Club Diversity on South High is in the other.

One would assume that with busy streetcars going up and down High Street in the early part of the twentieth century, shoppers, businessmen and children would not be expecting to see body parts in the dirt. Yet, every now and then, when a new foundation was being excavated, or a street widened, there they were, the bones of the long dead. And they just did not confine themselves to North High Street. They could be found as far away as Goodale Park. Who were these people?

The Old North Graveyard was easy to forget because it was mostly paved over. It was the city's first cemetery. When the city began in 1812, there was no churchyard or graveyard for the new town. There was one in Franklinton. A gift of land, in a wooded and sometimes swampy area, was given to the proprietors who helped to begin Columbus. One of them was John Kerr, also the second mayor of Columbus, born in Ireland. He was named the agent of the proprietor's association, and in April, 1813, he was given the deed to the borough of Columbus. Unfortunately, there were no officials yet for the borough, and the land was actually outside the city limits. This situation, pardon the pun, would come back to haunt everyone.

Therefore, almost nine hundred feet from Naghten (North Public Lane) and the northern most part of the city, the graveyard measured two hundred by three hundred feet, one and a half acres. The main road to the land ran closer to the river than today's High Street.

Bodies began to be buried here, but there were no official records and no official supervisory body though it was a city cemetery. In the 1820s, already containing bodies, the land was given to the city (officially) by Kerr and his wife for the sum of one dollar. This was to revert to Kerr's heirs if it ceased to be used for burials.

The documents are lost, but assume that more and more land was added to the graveyard over time. John Starr's farm, land from Lincoln Goodale and a purchase was made from old Colonel Doherty property to add land next to and along the Columbus-Worthington Pike (High Street). The graveyard had grown to seven acres. The Doherty family reserved for themselves some land beside an old beech tree for their own burials. Part of this new land was also to be laid out for free burial lots for the needy. Burials were to be done in chronological (not family) order, which seemed like a good idea since there was a cholera epidemic raging. This line of graves was cholera row. In a less-than racially sensitive time, a portion was set aside for "colored persons" who were to be buried by the city who paid the sexton—it was the same arrangement made if a stranger died in the city and needed to be buried. The city paid.

In 1834, regulations demanded that a fence was in order to keep the cows and pigs from rooting in the graves. Sites were available for five dollars. The sexton made two dollars per burial for anyone over fifteen years of age, and one dollar and fifty cents for those under the age. Few plots were recorded, and most records were not required to be organized or even written.

When the matter of messy accounting was taken seriously, it seems that almost all of the seven acres were full. The city opened a second burial site on Livingston Avenue (in front of Children's Hospital), which is sometimes called the South Cemetery and sometimes the East Cemetery.

In 1839, there was a report that eleven graves had been opened and eleven bodies stolen. Since Ohio State's medical school had not yet been created, it might be presumed that they had been taken by members of the Worthington Medical College. There was always a lively trade around such acquisitions. But free bodes were even better. The city hired a watchman and installed a new fence. Another seven acres were obtained from John and Cyrus Brickell, whose father had been an early settler. The graveyard was "maturing."

A small structure was erected (where Barley's is) to use as a death house—for preparation of bodies before burial. In 1848, not only were the Germans coming to town, but Green Lawn Cemetery was opening, and its first burials were cholera victims.

Boston, Cincinnati and other cities had stopped the practice of burying inside city limits and were being careful to not bury in areas where bodies could pollute the ground water. Many families wanted to keep the bodies of their loved ones in the North Graveyard, and though the city officially closed the cemetery, burials still occurred. Many of those buried had no living family members to look for them. Others who decided to rebury loved ones at Green Lawn (they were offering free plots to help make this adjustment) could not remember exactly where the burials were. One man, who had tended his father's grave over the years and was sure he knew exactly where to find him, was surprised to find a young man of a different race in the grave.

New fences to keep out the pigs and evildoers were a temporary measure, and then came the Civil War—who could do this now? The city continued to press to close the cemetery,

Constantly short of money, the city was tired of trying to respond to complaints, so when the Union Deport Company offered to buy the land in 1868 in order to expand the railroad tracks and deport, the city officials may have danced with joy to receive fifteen thousand dollars for a hundred

Bones and remnants of nineteenth-century burials have long haunted the bars and taverns of the Short North (in many ways). *EPA.*

feet of graves. Dead bodies, money, development, politics—sound like a familiar story? Kerr's heirs sued the city. Other lot owners sued the city, the railroads and the Doherty heirs on the argument for a right of easement. The city had prohibited burials but also did not keep the graveyard in good condition. The city just wanted to keep the money and settle the issue, In conclusion, Green Lawn offered free lots, the city paid for re-burials and 329 bodies were removed.

However, more bodies were found by accident in the 1880s and again in 1913. From 1922 to 1950, more bodies were found along Park Street. Sewer work in 2001 required an extensive survey. Bones, bodies, coffin nails, lead-head screws, medicinal bottles, cloth-covered iron buttons, pocket watch casings, grave handles and parts of children's coffins were found. Everybody out yet?

The story of the North Graveyard is the backdrop to the taverns of Barley's, Mac's, the Char-Bar, and possibly the Level, though it seems out of the original site—of course, without original records it is hard to determine. The Level, which has spirits that move the tables, has its own problems, being built in the former Old Time Religion Hall. The cornerstone indicates a 1920s building, and it is, but on the site of a 1911 home owned by the Wharton family. This home later became, yes, a saloon, though not before the house was owned by Otterbein College and later lived in by Mr. Starkey, a night watchman, and later by Mr. Burfield, an express messenger. Otterbein College in Westerville continued to own the site until 1932. Behind the house, the Hi-Lincoln Service Station also shared the property. In 1944, the building was the Remington Realty and later the Ohio Conference Methodist Church, and in 1946, it was the Old Time Religion Hall. The church was founded in 1929 but at another location. No wonder the spirits here are not just alcoholic.

Gradually, and with the elimination of the graveyard, homes turned over to businesses. Mac's is actually several buildings connected, and in the basement of the oldest portion, there is a deep basement with wooden partitions, very much like cribs (prostitution cribs, that is).

Barleys's is the major watering hole that is smack dab on the eastern side of the Old North Graveyard. It is part of the late nineteenth and early twentieth-century commercial building boom of post–Civil War Columbus. As one of the buildings in close proximity to the railroad, the building was long associated with furniture storerooms or warehouses. Most of the buildings were used by the Goodsell Brothers Furniture Company, the Columbus Furniture showroom, the Fournir Plumbing and Factory Supply and the Carlisle Furniture Company. The ghost sign of the furniture company was visible on the south face until the building of a new hotel covered the view of the wall. Up the street was the Wilcox Block, and this had also been the Advance Thresher Company and the Birdsell Manufacturing Company. It was another block before the first saloon appeared in 1911—Doyle's Saloon.

Char-Bar and the small white frame building immediately to the north of it have been on the site since the land was reclaimed from the North Graveyard. Both are interestingly detailed and frequently commented on. The small white-frame building is the Kuehner-Kohn Saloon and the oldest frame commercial building left on North High. It is distinctive, with its picket-like siding, and the history is traceable only to the 1880s, though it is considered the oldest frame commercial building still in existence on North High Street. In 1905, it was the Keuhner barbershop, which also made cigars. In 1911, it was May Brandy's saloon. Before World War I, it had become part of the Carlisle furniture company next door and remained that for decades.

The Char-Bar, its neighbor, was known for years as the Viaduct Restaurant, and with good reason. It was on the viaduct that carried the railroads under High Street, but it also lost a story. The basement of the building was once

A 1910 photo of North High Street looking south from the viaduct. The Char-Bar building can be seen on the left. *CML.*

the first floor, and a doorway at the bottom of the basement steps was the front door. Columbus's worst traffic nightmares involved the crossing of trains and other vehicles. After working on a number of solutions, including a tunnel for vehicles and an overpass for trains, the idea was reversed. The tunnel became fouled with horse droppings.

Standing at the blocked former front door, it is interesting to speculate on who came through and what the street might have been like (besides fouled). The most important visitor to come near was probably President Abraham Lincoln, but unfortunately, he was heading home for burial in Illinois. The county coroner, Patrick Egan, had his office and his funeral home only steps away, at 22 West Naghten Street. He had been entrusted with all the necessary procedures for keeping the body fresh. The upper floors of the Char-Bar were once rooming houses and offices. Here, Irish girls, including one Miss Annie O'Reilly, lived, and offices sold war bonds during World War I. In the 1890s, business came in and flew out with regularity—generally tradespeople. One listing was for Himmel van Rooyan and Muenshaft. A law firm? No, a tailor.

The present owner originally had the famed Char-Bar across from the Ohio State University—in fact there were two—and the other was around the corner on Fifteen Avenue. He also owned another restaurant on the East Side.

On the opposite side of High Street, Club Diversity's first use was, obviously a house, and what a house it was. Large and architecturally detailed for a wealthy family, it is amazing how many other connections it has to the history of Columbus. It was the home of Adolf Theobald, a German who made good in engineering, mining and, later, as president of the Columbus Edison Electric Company. In 1930, this company would become one of two hundred municipal electric companies that purchased and consolidated through Ohio Edison. By 1997, it became First Energy.

Theobald's house was on the main street of the German South Side (that was never known as German Village but rather Little Germany or South Side). Germans were not always the wealthy of the city, but they were thrifty. They had settled on land on the South Side, which was cheaper because

Located at 863 South High Street, Club Diversity is a popular lesbian, gay, bisexual and transgender (LGBT) hangout with live theater on the second floor and was once the mansion of a member of city council. *SB*.

it was downstream on the river. The Germans wanted the appearance of order. No barking dogs, no loose daughters, no rowdy children.

Across the street, in an era before Plank's restaurant, was Druid Hall, which gave accommodation to an amazing assortment of organizations. The list is very Teutonic, sometimes humorous, but instructive as to how many groups it takes to build a community—the Columbus Grove Concordia

Club Diversity, 863 South High Street, as seen today. *TB*.

Circle, the Franklin County Chapter of the UAOD (?), the Athena Court and Order of the Pharoahs, the Brotherhood of the Railroad Machine Workers, the First Ward of the Democratic Club, the International Bookbinders Union, the Brewery Workers Union, the Maritime Social Club (possibly connected with Buckeye Lake), the Brewery Workers Union and the Union Burma Social Club. The last two groups were in Druid Hall even into the 1940s, after the Theobald house was already changing.

Germans did not come to Columbus to be farmers—they were merchants, craftsmen, skilled or hoping-to-be-skilled workers. In addition to working for a brewery, many men worked in the shoe factories. There were sometimes as many as eight large shoe factories operating in any decade. Because Columbus was a transportation crossroads and shoes were something everyone needed and wanted, one out of every five pairs of shoes worn in the United States was made in Columbus. Others say one out of every eight pairs of shoes is the correct statistic. Columbus even made burial shoes, nicely detailed and designed to fit a variety of corpses. They were not for traveling (obviously). They were made of heavy paper, and a pair, occasionally, will turn up at a flea market or an antique show—lovely shoes, not for rainy days, wrapped in tissue and in a box marked "burial shoes."

The Theobalds also owned the MacDonald Foundry, and their son, Paul, was a 1908 graduate of Ohio State with degrees in engineering and draftsmanship. Paul worked for Carnegie Steel and wrote reports for Edward Orton, first Ohio State president and first state geologist.

By the late 1940s, the Theobalds had downsized, and the house was turned into four (sometimes five) large apartments. The family had degrees, ambition and high social standing in the community (Adolph was also a city councilman), and he and his son owned a small wholesale liquor business. By Prohibition, the business had grown into a large stone building on South High—but all was liquidated with the coming enforcement of the law, and much money was lost. Strange that they built a liquor business and lost it all, only to have their house eventually become a tavern.

The large apartments were rented to a variety of people—single men who worked as guards at the Ohio Penitentiary and married men, musicians, who had wives but no children. That the pattern is so consistent in occupation and goes on for so many years, it might be assumed that they were all friends who worked together. When the bartender of Club Diversity, now a quiet bar that welcomes a diverse group as the name implies, mentioned disturbances, such as the jukebox that would come on by itself, it seemed another urban legend. However, a medium provided a name for a woman who seemed to be the music lover, and historical research done independently of even knowing this confirmed a woman with that name as living in the house in the 1940s.

It may not be fair to end with a mystery, but good history and good tours should make people think. Columbus Landmark Foundation's tours and programs stress that curiosity is lifelong learning. There is more out there than one can imagine, Horatio, and it underscores how important it is to connect stories to objects and humanity to architecture.

The last photo is a building that did not start out to be a tavern, an inn, a saloon or a coffeehouse. Its purpose was to house businesses of the

Home Furnishing Company, at 239 South Fourth Street. Current location of Little Palace. *CML.*

first generation of retail merchandisers who left their fathers' pushcarts behind. As Jewish merchants, they joined the family tradition of innovative and hardworking entrepreneurs. The building had been owned by the Hinterschieds. Max Polster purchased it, and his brother Louis owned the store next door. Another brother named Morris owned a similar shop nearby. Their father had owned a scrap and junkyard, unfortunately situated close to the Donaldson Street synagogue (now gone), and a relative admitted that it was a hard place to concentrate on prayers with the inevitable banging next door.

Over time, the building was associated with the selling of Queensware (to be left a mystery), a Krogers Grocery and Bakery, a home furnishings store, Omar the baker, a shoe shop, a rummage store, a Dolly Madison Little Cakes bakery, an auction house, a thrift store for Children's Hospital and part of the Annex Hotel, which rented to single men, widows and retirees. Its closest connection to taverns or saloons was that one of its renters was a lady bartender in the 1940s.

Where is it? What is it? Who built it? What changed it? Whose lives were bound up in a building that many might have thought unremarkable, if not ugly? This is not a contest. There are no prizes for finding out what bar it became. It is an example and a challenge to more fully realize Columbus's taverns and saloons, like all Columbus buildings and architecture, connect us to others whose lives and times are unremarkably remarkable.

Epilogue

A book on vintage taverns, inns, saloons and a historic hotel and club should end with a toast or several.

The Athletic Club of Columbus, famous for its classic period cocktails, has contributed recipes to salute and celebrate important anniversaries this year: Columbus Landmarks Foundation turns 35, the Athletic Club of Columbus turns 100, the Westin Great Southern turns 115 and the City of Columbus turns 200.

Here's to your foundations, windows, doors and materials. May they always stand, shine, open and shelter the buildings that house our stories, our history and our collective memory

Courtesy of the Athletic Club of Columbus

French Connection
1.5 ounces of Courvoisier
1.5 ounces of Grand Marnier
Neat and served heated in a brandy snifter.

Manhattan Perfect
2.5 ounces bourbon
1.5 ounces of sweet vermouth
1.5 ounces dry vermouth, and 3 dashes of bitters
Traditionally served chilled and neat in a martini glass. Traditional garnish is a cherry wrapped with an orange peel creating a flag.

Side Car

1.5 ounces VSOP Cognac

.75 ounce Cointreau

.75 ounce fresh lemon juice

Traditionally served chilled and neat in a martini glass with an orange wheel for garnish. Many substitute vanilla oak-aged Armagnac for the Cognac to soften and enhance the cocktail.

Aged in Wood. The end of Prohibition caught state government unprepared. *Illustration by Billy Ireland, OSUCL and CD.*

Bibliography

Newspapers

Columbus Citizen Journal
Columbus Dispatch
Columbus Evening Dispatch
Columbus Star
Ohio State Journal
Western Intelligencer

Books

Alexiou, Alice Sparberg. *The Flatiron: The New York Landmark and the Incomparable City that Rose with It*. New York: St. Martin's Press, 2010.

Bash, Ramck & Co. *Franklin County Directory*. Westerville, OH: Bash, Ramck & Co., 1898.

City of Columbus. Department of Development. *North Market Area Columbus, Ohio Rebilitation Feasibility Study Summary*. City of Columbus Department of Development, January 21, 1980.

City of Columbus. Ohio Environmental Agency. *Date Recovery Conducted at Impacted Locations within the former North Graveyard in the North Market District*. City of Columbus. Franklin County, Ryan Weller and Weller Associates, 2004.

Cole, Charles, Jr. *A Fragile Capital: Identity and the Early Years of Columbus, Ohio*. Columbus: Ohio State University, 2001.

Columbus First Presbyterian Church. *One Hundredth Anniversary.* Columbus, 1905.

Custodio, Brenda, and Brenda Dutton. *Franklinton: History and Heritage.* Franklinton Historical Society. Columbus, OH: Inkwell, 1997.

Ervin, Mary D. *Ohio Woman's Christian Temperance Union: Historic Highlights, Diamond Jubilee Anniversary, 1874–1949.* Columbus, OH: Ohio Women's Christian Temperance Union, 1949.

Foster, David Wayne. *A Brief History of the Breweries of German Village.* Columbus, OH: self-published, 1987.

Foster, Emily, ed. *The Ohio Frontier: An Anthology of Early Readings.* Lexington: University Press of Kentucky, 1996.

Garrett, Betty, with Edward R. Lentz. *Columbus: America's Crossroads.* Tulsa, OK: Continental Heritage Press, 1980.

Hart, R. Douglas. *The Ohio Frontier: Crucible of the Old Northwest, 1720–1830.* Bloomington: Indiana University Press, 1996.

Hoster, Jay, and Christine Hayes. *The Ben Hayes Scrapbook.* Columbus, OH: Ravine Books, 1991.

Lathrop, Elise. *Early American Inns and Taverns.* New York: Tudor Publishing Company, 1926.

Lee, Alfred E., *History of the City of Columbus.* 2 vols. New York: Munsell, 1992.

Lentz, Ed. *As It Were: Stories of Old Columbus.* 2 vols. N.p.: Redmountain Press, 1998 and 2001.

Macabe, Lida Rose. *Don't You Remember?* Columbus, OH: A.H. Smythe, 1884.

Maennerchor. *Die Geschichte des Columbus Maennerchors.* Self-published, 1948.

Mariani, John. *America Eats Out.* New York: William Morrow and Company, 1991.

Martin, William. *History of Franklin County.* Columbus, OH: Follett, Foster, 1884.

Maxwell, Fay. *History of German Village.* Columbus, OH: self-published, n.d.

Monkkonen, Eric H. *The Dangerous Class: Crime and Poverty in Columbus, Ohio, 1860–1885.* Cambridge, MA: Harvard University Press, 1975.

Ohio Historical Records Survey Project, Service Division Works Project Administration. *Inventory of the County Archives of Ohio. No. 25 Franklin County.* Columbus, OH: 1942.

Okrent, Daniel. *Last Call: The Rise and Fall of Prohibition.* New York: Scribner, 2010.

Polk, R.L. & Co. *Franklin County Directory for 1893*, vol. III. Columbus, OH: R.L. Polk & Co., 1893 and vol. IV, 1896–1897.

Schlegel, Donald. *The Columbus City Graveyards*. Columbus, OH: Columbus History Service, 1985.

Sismondo, Christine. *America Walks into a Bar*. New York: Oxford University Press, 2011.

Sittler, Margaret. "The German Element in Columbus Before the Civil War." Master's thesis. Columbus: Ohio State University, 1932.

Upton, Dell, and John Michael Vlach, ed. *Common Places: Readings in American Vernacular Architecture*. Athens: University of Georgia Press, 1986.

Weisenburger, Francis Phelps. *Columbus During the Civil War*. Columbus: Ohio State University Press, 1963.

White, Ruth. *We Too Built Columbus*. Columbus, OH: Stoneman Press, 1936.

Wooley, Charles, and Barbara Van Brimmer. *The Second Blessing: Columbus Medicine and Health—The Early Years*. Columbus, OH: Columbus Medical Association Foundation and the Medical Heritage Center, 2006.

Yoder, Paton. *Taverns and Travellers*. Bloomington: Indiana University Press, 1969.

About the Authors

om Betti serves on the board of Columbus Landmarks Foundation and is also chair of the Education Committee charged with leading the organization's educational tours and extensive programming. He is dedicated to bringing history to life through entertaining storytelling. He co-leads the Historic Tavern Tours with Doreen, bringing dry humor and wit. Tom also founded and leads the Historic Preservation Committee of the Athletic Club

of Columbus, celebrating, organizing and documenting the club's one-hundred-year history. A native of the Cleveland, Ohio, area, it is fitting that his condo resides in the historic 1898 Hartman Hotel Building in Columbus, Ohio, where he lives with his Boston terrier, Hugo.

oreen Uhas Sauer serves as Board President for Columbus Landmarks Foundation and on a number of boards in the University District, where she is active in historic preservation, urban issues and local history. A longtime Columbus educator with Columbus City Schools, she currently directs a Teaching American History grant and has worked extensively in international

civic education. She has received statewide recognition for her work in preservation education, developed more than thirty local history/architecture programs and was named Ohio Teacher of the Year in 2003. She has coauthored books on local Columbus history and on the University District, where she resides with her husband, John, whose roots are extensive in the German South Side.

Visit us at
www.historypress.net